MY DAILY DISCOVERMENT

40 Days of Vocational Discernment for Young Adults

ANDREW HYDE

 FriesenPress

One Printers Way
Altona, MB R0G 0B0
Canada

www.friesenpress.com

Copyright © 2021 by Andrew Hyde
First Edition — 2021

Unless otherwise indicated, scripture quotations are from the New Revised Standard Version Bible, copyright © 1989 the Division of Christian Education of the National Council of the Churches of Christ in the United States of America. Used by permission. All rights reserved.

Scripture quotations marked NIV are from The Holy Bible, New International Version®, NIV® Copyright © 1973, 1978, 1984, 2011 by Biblica, Inc.® Used by permission. All rights reserved worldwide.

Scripture quotations marked NLT are taken from the Holy Bible, New Living Translation, copyright © 1996, 2004, 2015 by Tyndale House Foundation. Used by permission of Tyndale House Publishers, Inc., Carol Stream, Illinois 60188. All rights reserved.

Scripture quotations marked MSG are taken from THE MESSAGE, copyright © 1993, 2002, 2018 by Eugene H. Peterson. Used by permission of NavPress. All rights reserved. Represented by Tyndale House Publishers, Inc.

A previous version of Kimberly Ivany's reflection titled, "A Difficult Decision" appeared as "A Fork in the Road" in Salvationist (October 23, 2015) https://salvationist.ca/articles/2015/10/isjc-internship/ and is used here by author's permission.

Copyright © Henri Nouwen. Excerpt from *Life of the Beloved* by Henri Nouwen (Crossroad, 2002). Reprinted by arrangement with The Crossroad Publishing Company. www.crossroadpublishing.com

All rights reserved.

No part of this publication may be reproduced in any form, or by any means, electronic or mechanical, including photocopying, recording, or any information browsing, storage, or retrieval system, without permission in writing from FriesenPress.

ISBN
978-1-03-911758-7 (Hardcover)
978-1-03-911757-0 (Paperback)
978-1-03-911759-4 (eBook)

1. RELIGION, CHRISTIAN LIFE, CALLING & VOCATION

Distributed to the trade by The Ingram Book Company

Table of Contents

v	Introduction
19	Who is God? Knowing the character of God Days 1 - 4
45	Who am I? Knowing my own belovedness Days 5 – 8
73	What does God do? Exploring God's work in the world Days 9 - 12
101	What am I called to do? Listening for my vocational call Days 13 – 27
195	How do I make decisions? Discerning between different opportunities Days 28 – 36
259	How do I live the decisions I make? Reflecting the character of God every day Days 37 – 40
283	A Final Blessing and Commission Get on with it!

Introduction

At age 26, Josiah has been King of Israel for 8 years already. It is not an enviable role—there are different demands and advisors and schools of thought pulling him in all directions. He is trying to be faithful to God, but he doesn't really know how. Then, one day, a worker he hired to renovate the temple come to him with an amazing find—a book, containing the lost writings of Moses, the first five books of today's Hebrew scriptures (2 Kings 22). What a discoverment! Through those writings, Josiah hears the loving direction of God, and it guides him for the rest of his reign as king.

A rural teenager named Mary is given an extraordinary task. "You will conceive in your womb and bear a son, and you will name him Jesus" (Luke 1:31). And though this unexpected turn throws a wrench in Mary's plans, she responds in obedience, by trusting in God. When visiting her older cousin Elizabeth, Mary realizes she does not walk this path alone. Elizabeth has received a similar calling and is a few months further along than Mary. What a discoverment! As the two cousins live into God's purposes for them, they draw strength and courage and wisdom from each other.

A recent graduate of a prestigious school, Saul was being fast-tracked for a leadership position in the religious sector. Having completed an internship— where he learned the basics in keeping religious minorities at bay— he is now being trusted to lead a few projects on his own. His mentors can see great things in Saul's future. But on the commute to his next big assignment, Saul has a vision of the risen Christ that disrupts his upward trajectory. He is disarmed by a single, pointed question. "Saul, Saul. Why do you persecute me?" (Acts 9:4). Saul can't respond. Why indeed, has he chosen this path? How has he ended up here? Is this really what he wants to be doing with the rest of his life? What a discoverment! After having his life turned upside down, Saul finds a new community, new wisdom, and a new purpose worth committing his life to, and it changes the course of the world for millions.

A discoverment is a moment of clarity that helps orient our lives. It's a revealing of something unknown. An uncovering of something hidden. A discoverment is an 'a-ha' moment or an epiphany that shows us something of who we are and the role we play in this complex and mysterious world.

Discoverments can sometimes drop from the sky. They can hit like a bolt of lightning, or waft as naturally and easily as the breeze on a summer day. Just as often though, discoverments are the fruit of some hard inner work, and they result from a process of asking good questions, gathering precious wisdom, and embodying new postures. This workbook is a guide to that second kind of discoverment, the kind born by a process.

If you are looking for direction in life, if you're asking important questions about school, careers, relationships, etc. and you come seeking answers, this workbook may very well disappoint you. This workbook will not give you a lot of answers. This workbook, instead, hopes to give you a framework–especially if you are a young person trying to live in the way of Jesus—for a lifetime of discoverments, tools for the work of vocational discernment, some bones upon which you might flesh out a sense of meaning and purpose for your life. It does so by asking some important questions:

Who is God?
Who am I?
What does God do?
What am I called to do?
How do I make faithful decisions?
How do I live into the decisions I make?

Each question is accompanied by a handful of daily reflections that I share from my perspective and faith journey. Some of them draw on stories of my own childhood and experience. Some of them are born out of the many conversations I've been privileged to be part of in my role as a campus minister at the University of Guelph. There are 40 reflections altogether—which fits well into a season of discernment and learning—but these are by no means the only 40 things worth considering. Each question could spawn dozens more, and perhaps you will spiral out into some new questions, wonderings, or critiques over the course of your reading. There is space for your own journalling, doodles, prayers, and reflections—and those are really the most valuable part of this process. There are also some additional reflections from some of my friends and colleagues, people with a breadth of experience and vocational insights to share. I trust that you will find their wisdom a real blessing to receive, just as I have.

It is my prayer that this process—and the little community you find in these pages—will open up some new perspectives on your life, guide you into deeper relationship with the Divine, and equip you to ask good questions of the life you are living.

Life.

What a gift to discover. What a blessing to share. What a responsibility to steward wisely.

May you sense God's presence in your life over these next 40 days. May you hear God's call in the discoverments ahead.

Andrew Hyde
University of Guelph

About the Author:

Andrew Hyde is the Ecumenical Campus Minister at the University of Guelph. A Designated Lay Minister in the United Church of Canada, Andrew has served in a variety of youth and young adult ministry contexts—including camps, congregations, presbyteries, and university chaplaincy—since 2001. Andrew lives with his wife Andrea and their two children in Guelph, Ontario—within the Between the Lakes Purchase (Treaty 3) and on the treaty lands of the Mississaugas of the Credit.

The **Ecumenical Campus Ministry** is the home of the Anglican, Presbyterian, and United Church at the University of Guelph. All proceeds from this sale of this workbook go to sustaining and growing ECM's vital ministry at the UofG. To learn more about ECM's ministry, visit www.ECMguelph.org.

To access additional resources, such as the Discoverment Group Study Guide and additional reflections, visit www.discoverment.org.

List of Contributors:

Katie Thomson Aitken is a Naturopathic Doctor, author, and founder of the Tranquil Minds Anxiety Programs. She believes that when each of us cultivates peace in our hearts, we can create peace in our world. Katie lives in Guelph, Ontario where she is an active member of her local church congregation. Visit her website at www.tranquilmindnaturopath.com.

Mitchell Anderson serves as lead minister at St. Paul's United Church in Saskatoon, Saskatchewan. His journey following Jesus began in high school when he realized he was gay, which led him to the United Church of Canada. Mitchell is dënesułiné with Cree and Métis ancestry, and lives in Saskatoon with his partner, Jordan.

Morgan Bell is a candidate for ordered ministry in The United Church of Canada and a PhD student at Emmanuel College, University of Toronto. He hails from Omemee, Ontario and has served in youth ministry, pulpit supply, and on the Roman Catholic-United Church National Dialogue. When not reading and writing, he can be found making music, cooking food, or curled up watching movies.

Johannes Chan is a human being who likes roaming around trees and rivers, reading books, and writing. Once an engineering and international development student, Johannes now works keeping people's electricity under control. Johannes lives in Mississauga, Ontario. To read Johannes' blog, visit https://encephalonfatigue.tumblr.com.

Cam Fraser lives in Regina, Saskatchewan on Traditional Nêhiyawak, Anihsināpēk, Dakota, Lakota and Nakoda Territory, the homeland of the Métis/Michif Nation (Treaty 4). With his spouse and 3 children, he is the Minister at Knox-Metropolitan United Church. He likes to read, play board games, is a rookie bird watcher, and an aspiring banjo player.

Leanne Friesen is a pastor, mother, speaker and writer living in Hamilton, Ontario where she serves as Lead Minister of Mount Hamilton Baptist Church. Her congregation self-describes as a small, regular church of regular people, who keep seeing extraordinary things because—Jesus. You can read Leanne's blog at www.leannefriesen.com.

Tianna Gocan recently graduated as a Bachelor of Science from the University of Waterloo in Waterloo, Ontario. She is currently undergoing the discernment process for ministry in the Anglican Church of Canada. She's an active member in her local parish and in her spare time enjoys reading, writing, and yoga.

Andrea Hyde is a high school teacher and guidance counsellor with the Halton District School Board. She lives in Guelph, Ontario with her husband Andrew and their two children. She is passionate about equity and diversity in education, and enjoys her early morning runs, drinking tea, and cuddles with her beagle puppy, Oakley.

Kimberly Ivany is a world-travelling, deep-feeling, CBC journalist in Toronto, Ontario. She is passionate about people and telling their stories, as well as dancing—in any form. If she's not in the studio, or holding the government to account through her work, you can find Kimberly encountering the whimsical Mystery in her city.

Alana Martin lives in Toronto, Ontario with her dog Murphy. A new commissioned Diaconal Minister, Alana started working with The GO Project when she was 19, and never left! Now as the Minister to GO, she finds her joy in creating innovative, engaging and meaningful discernment programs for children and youth in the United Church of Canada.

Robin McGauley is an artist, spiritual director, and ordained minister in The United Church of Canada. She became a Veriditas Certified Labyrinth Facilitator in 2011 after training with Lauren Artress and has led countless presentations, workshops, retreats on the labyrinth. Visit her website at www.robinmcgauley.com.

Karen Orr is a spiritual director from Elmira, Ontario. She also serves as ministry staff person for the Youth Ministry at St. Andrew's Presbyterian Church in Kitchener, Ontario. Karen helped create the original Discoverment small group curriculum and co-developed the Encounters program of group spiritual direction for youth.

Margaret Propp was born and raised in Calgary, Alberta. Born to immigrant parents, Margaret is Nisei second generation Japanese-Canadian. Ordained in the Evangelical Lutheran Church in Canada, she currently serves Lutheran Campus Ministry (University of Calgary) as chaplain, and as pastor of Historic Trinity Lutheran Church in Calgary.

Ben Reid-Howells is a transnational community organizer who believes that globally connected, locally enacted community-led direct action is a powerful means of regeneration. Son of Scottish/English immigrants he identifies with both colonized and colonizer and strives to connect community initiatives across Turtle Island and beyond to co-create resilient, shared futures.

Alydia Smith is a worship leader, educator, caregiver, and Jesus-follower who serves as Program Coordinator for Worship, Music and Spirituality for The United Church of Canada. She is a tuba player who holds a bachelor's in music from Western University, a master's in divinity from the Atlantic School of Theology, and a doctorate in worship from Drew University.

Romario Smith is a studio art student at the University of Guelph, where he also serves as the coordinator of that campus' Queer Christian Community. Born in Jamaica and now living in Ajax, Ontario, Romario provided the illustrations that mark each section of this workbook. To view more of Romario's work, follow him on Instagram at @we_are_starving.

Who is God?

Knowing the character of God
Days 1 - 4

SET YOUR INTENTION: WHO IS GOD?

In this first section of reflections, I want to invite you to consider the character of God—how you know it, how you articulate it, and how you have been (and continue to be) formed by it. We'll consider the nature of God, mystery and revelation, what we can hold onto and what we must let go of.

It may feel like a slow way to get into our considerations of the future, your vocational calling, and the work of decision-making. I get it. It is tempting to want to jump forward. But I hope you'll discover that having a sense of who God is—of knowing God more deeply and maturely—is foundational for those other considerations. You will be well served by rooting your vocational discernment in the character of God.

Consider:

- What am I hoping to discover as I engage this question of who God is?
- What pressing questions or desires might I need to set aside to be present in this moment?
- What are my initial thoughts or impressions when I begin to think about the character of God?

Let's Pray:

Gracious God, you are beyond comprehension and beyond perfect description. Yet you are not unknown to your Creation. Attend to me as I begin to consider and discover anew who you truly are. Give me insight to perceive you as you really are in my life, not as others claim you to be. Make me attentive to your revealed self and grant me peace as I encounter the mystery of your ways. Just as I am discovering who I am, let me know a little of who you are and how we might walk through life together. In Jesus' name I pray. Amen.

www.discoverment.org

DAY 1

Milk and Stones

> Like newborn infants, long for the pure, spiritual milk, so that by it you may grow into salvation — if indeed you have tasted that the Lord is good. Come to him, a living stone, though rejected by mortals yet chosen and precious in God's sight, and like living stones, let yourselves be built into a spiritual house, to be a holy priesthood, to offer spiritual sacrifices acceptable to God through Jesus Christ.
>
> 1 Peter 2:2-5

A first taste of something—whether it's a new cuisine, a lover's lips, or a newfound freedom—is a precious thing to experience and hold onto.

I remember my first taste of coffee. I was nine years old, sitting in the stands of Ivor Wynne Stadium with my family, watching the Hamilton Tiger-Cats play Canadian football against the Saskatchewan Roughriders. It was a bitterly cold and rainy autumn night. At halftime, my father went down to the concession stand and upon finding the vendors out of hot chocolate, procured me a cup of coffee, loaded with cream and sugar, to get something warm into my shivering belly.

I won't say I recall my first taste of coffee being a delicious one—not when I was expecting hot chocolate with marshmallows—but its warmth was good, and I appreciated the trust placed in me to partake of such an adult beverage. It felt like I was being welcomed into a new phase of life.

Since then, my taste for—and possible dependence on—coffee has developed. Not to the point where I am an aficionado or expert or anything like that, but to the point where I can indeed appreciate the goodness that is my morning cup, and articulate with confidence what it is about coffee that I like and how I like it. Medium roast. Double double. Tim Horton's instead of Starbucks. Oskie-wee-wee all the way.

Likewise, I can recall my first tastes of the Lord's goodness in my life. They came to me in the warm nurture of my Sunday School teachers as a child. They came to me in the enthusiastic encouragement of my camp counsellors each summer at church camp. They came to me in the quiet moments with my red pocket Bible as I stared at the moon from my childhood bedroom.

First tastes are precious. First tastes are memorable. First tastes can feel good and comforting, exhilarating and warm, when the world outside feels rainy and isolating and cold. Many of you who are reading this book, are doing it because somehow, somewhere, you got a first and early taste of the Lord's goodness in your life.

But tastes change over time. Palettes develop. Tastebuds change and grow and mature. We may age into deeper appreciation, or finer articulation of our experiences and our truths, or we may abandon certain tastes for ones we deem better.

Likewise, in the life of faith, as we grow and deepen and develop our dependence on the Divine, we gain new language and use new imagery to describe the goodness we find in God. From the language of milk and thirsty infants, we develop towards stories of stones and houses, images we can build a life on, that will see us into new chapters of living. Images and language that call us to be a holy priesthood and to live sacrificially. Images and stories that include things like rejection and work and other hard things that adults have to deal with on the daily.

When I was little, our family used to pray at every meal the familiar words: "God is great. God is good. Let us thank Him for our food."

To this day, I affirm the goodness and the greatness of God. Yet the language I've developed to articulate the greatness and the goodness of God is more precise, more nuanced, more full-bodied, and tested against my experience. My concept of God is a little less gendered, a little more generous, relies on fewer generalizations, and is—I pray—a little more generative than the theological sippy cups of my childhood.

Words like great and good are the theological milk I was brought up on. But in order to build a life, I've had to begin thinking of God as more than that. How many people, I wonder, have walked away from faith because they are trying to build a life on child-sized theology?

As you engage in this process towards vocational discernment, I encourage you to hold onto the truths of God that gave you a first taste of divine goodness. But at the same time, may you grow them into something more substantial, more nuanced, more sophisticated—something you can build a life upon. Something that will serve you, and the world around you, well.

Questions for Reflection:

Where did you first taste the goodness of God? Describe your experience of encountering God's goodness for the first time. Who are the people, the communities, the voices, that gave you that gift?

What language did you first use to understand who God was? Does that language still serve you well? What about it do you want to hold onto? What about it is beginning to feel like it doesn't fit?

How has your language about God changed? What language is emerging for you as you mature in faith and know God more deeply?

In the Hebrew scriptures, the young prophet Isaiah tastes the forgiveness of the Lord for the first time, when an angel touches a coal to his lips. The Lord then asks, "Whom shall I send? Who shall go for us?" to which Isaiah replies, "Here am I. Send me!" (Isaiah 6:8). In what ways does a growing understanding of God open us up to being used for God's purposes? What are the connections you see between spiritual formation and vocational discernment?

DAY 2

Mystery's Shore

Come now, you who say, "Today or tomorrow we will go to such and such a town and spend a year there, doing business and making money." Yet you do not even know what tomorrow will bring. What is your life? For you are a mist that appears for a little while and then vanishes.

Instead you ought to say, "If the Lord wishes, we will live and do this or that."

James 4:13-15

When I was a child, our family used to spend summers at a cottage on the north shore of Lake Erie. If you've never stood on the shore of one of the Great Lakes, they are majestic inland seas, which stirred my imagination and gave me a sense of how big the universe was. There was something about standing on that rocky shore, with the waves crashing and the fishy smell of seaweed in the air—something about the watery horizon meeting the sky, and the endless expanse of stars at night—that opened me up to the mysteries of God and the possibilities of life.

How big was God and how vast was God's love for us? In my imagination, it was as vast as a Great Lake spread out before me.

The other amazing thing about our summer location, was that on a really clear day... a day without clouds, when the air pressure was just right... you could catch a faint glimpse, trace a dim outline, of the hills on the American side of the lake. Somewhere over there was Erie, Pennsylvania—which I realize now is a little less remarkable than my childhood imagination made it out to be—from which emanated the two American TV channels that, again on a clear day, we could sometimes pick up with the rabbit ear antenna on our cottage TV set. From that mysterious, far-off land I could occasionally pick up shows like "Saved By the Bell" and "Transformers," which I devoured because of their novelty if not because of their brilliance.

Anyone who takes time to faithfully consider their future, I believe, is standing at the edge of a great mystery. Think of all the possibilities. Think of all the opportunities. Think of all the adventure and hardship and challenges that might be waiting for you.

It is beautiful and intimidating, and exciting and scary, to stand so close to life's mysteries—to have the waves of God's presence lapping at your toes. It is holy ground indeed.

Yet from the other side of that mystery, cresting the horizon of divine possibility, sometimes… just sometimes… the Creator reveals to us little glimpses. Glimpses of who God is, glimpses of who we are called to become, glimpses of what a meaningful and abundant life can look like, and how we might be called to serve. Glimpses of a coming kingdom.

The church I belong to affirms, "We witness to Holy Mystery that is Wholly Love" (Song of Faith). Note that it's a holy mystery, that is entirely love—not the other way around. God is mostly, but not entirely, a mystery. Because of God's revelation to us, the glimpses we receive of who God is and what God is doing in the world, we can with confidence describe God as 100% love.

When we consider the future and seek to discover where God is calling us, we stand at the edge of a vast and holy mystery. Take a moment to breathe it in. But don't let mystery's vastness overwhelm you, for we are not kept entirely in a fog. God reveals to us just what we need to create a life that is made of purpose and meaning and love.

As you consider your future, may you stand on the edge of this mystery with God, attentive to the conditions around you, anticipating the next clear day when we might catch a glimpse of what God wants to show you.

Questions for Reflection:

How do you feel when you begin thinking about your future? Name some of the emotions that come over you.

When have you felt yourself close to the Holy Mystery that is Wholly Love? Have you ever caught a glimpse of something you felt God was revealing to you? What was it?

Read the story of Moses and the burning bush (Exodus 3:1-12). What does Moses' experience of standing on holy ground have in common with your own experience of considering your future?

Now read the story of Moses being hidden in the cleft of the rock from the Lord (Exodus 33:18-23). Why do you think God keeps some things hidden from us? How do you respond to the times when answers to your questions or responses to your longings have remained hidden from you?

DAY 3

The Big Reveal

> At that time Jesus said, "I thank you, Father, Lord of heaven and earth, because you have hidden these things from the wise and the intelligent and have revealed them to infants; yes, Father, for such was your gracious will. All things have been handed over to me by my Father; and no one knows the Son except the Father, and no one knows the Father except the Son and anyone to whom the Son chooses to reveal him."
>
> Matthew 11:25-27

At our house, we are suckers for all the home renovation shows on TV.

You know the ones—where they take a dilapidated old house or an out-of-date condominium and fix it up on behalf of some hard-on-their-luck but well-deserving family. Throughout the course of the show, you'll see all sorts of dramas: unexpected mould in the basement, differences of opinions among designers, or some kind of crack in the foundation that puts the whole project over budget and the renovation into jeopardy. And amidst all the drama, we get little glimpses of what the final renovation will look like—things like the colour palette, or pieces of furniture, or the possibility (and emotional release) that comes with knocking down the occasional wall or two.

But the highlight of these shows—the climax of each episode and the payoff for enduring every scintillating drama—is the big reveal at the end. This is where the contractors and designers get to show off their handiwork to the homeowners and to us viewers, with all the made-for-TV pauses, tears, and ooo's and awww's that follow. The big reveal is the point in the show that you don't want to miss. This is what makes these shows so addictive.

In the Christian story, we affirm that God reveals God's self to us in little glimpses when we faithfully engage things like Creation, scripture, our Christian tradition, reason, our experiences of the Holy Spirit, and even people of another (or no) faith, particularly those on the margins.

But we also affirm that the big reveal moment in God's story comes in the person of Jesus. If we want to see God's character, God's hopes for us, God's designs for our future, we as Christians look, first and foremost, to Jesus Christ. For it's in Jesus that we see God most fully revealed to us, and it's in Jesus that we place our hope.

So we pay attention to Jesus—to what he taught, to what he did, and particularly to what Jesus says about himself.

In John's gospel, Jesus gifts us with a number of "I am" statements, that help reveal to us who he is and what God is like. They are:

I am the Light of the World	*John 8:12*
I am the Bread of Life	*John 6::35-51*
I am the Sheep Gate	*John 10:7-10*
I am the Good Shepherd	*John 10:11-16*
I am the Way, the Truth, and the Life	*John 14:5-7*
I am the Resurrection and the Life	*John 11:23-27*

Jesus is like a light, revealing truth and beauty in the world. Jesus is a vine, providing connection and life to others. Jesus is like bread, nourishing all who partake. Jesus is a gate, offering security and safe passage. Jesus is like a shepherd, laying down his life for those he cares for. Jesus is the way, the path to the new, true, and beautiful life God has prepared for us—a life that cannot be bound by death or other complications. Jesus reveals God's character like no other.

As you take time to look up these statements, to read and meditate on them, ask God to reveal some new aspect of God's own self to you. If you've never done so before, take the time to read at least one of the Gospels (Matthew, Mark, Luke, or John) all the way through. Immerse yourself in the person and story of Jesus. See if there is something there that you can build your life on.

Questions for Reflection:

What are your first memories, your first impressions, of Jesus? How did you used to think of Jesus? How has your sense of Jesus changed or grown over the years?

What aspects of God's character do you see revealed in the "I am" statements of Jesus? Which statements resonate for you or spark your imagination? Which "I am" statements are you less sure of?

How does what you see in Jesus jive with what you know of God through other means (Creation, scripture, tradition, reason, experience, others, etc.)? What do you see in Jesus that is worth building a life upon?

If we claim that Jesus is the fullest revelation we have of God, why do you think that so many Christians find Christ-likeness to be so difficult? What might change in the world if more Christians actually behaved like Jesus and took the things he taught seriously?

4 WAYS OF LISTENING FOR GOD
by Morgan Bell

Crack open your Bible. God speaks to Hagar, to Moses, to Israel. In Jesus, God speaks to Mary (all of them!), to Peter, to his disciples. The Spirit speaks to Paul, to John, to the church. God won't stop talking! So, what do we do with all that noise? How do we know what God is saying? Christians have long wondered about this—and still do! A speaking God requires a discerning church.

One approach to discernment is the Wesleyan Quadrilateral. The quadrilateral describes the method that the founder of Methodism, John Wesley, used in his theology. (Wesley never actually spelled this out for himself, but don't let facts get in the way!) In this model, we can begin to understand the Almighty's will through scripture, tradition, reason, and experience. We can discern how God speaks to us today.

Scripture is fairly straightforward—it's the Bible! The Spirit uses the Word to witness to God by telling us what God has done, is doing, and will do. The Bible is like a pair of glasses that we wear so that we may see who God is and what God is doing in the world. In my church we believe, per A Song of Faith, that "the Spirit breathes revelatory power into scripture, bestowing upon it a unique and normative place in the life of the community" (Song of Faith). For Christians, scripture is both the foundational and final witness to our loving, liberating, and life-giving God.

Tradition is a little trickier. Tradition… isn't that why at Christmas we have to eat that Jello salad which no one actually likes? Not quite. Here, tradition refers to what the church has taught throughout the centuries, how we have read the scriptures, what we confess about our Christian faith. Tradition is what has been handed on to us by our forebears in faith: creeds and books and hymns and interpretations and lives well lived in the service of God. Tradition is the lens the church provides to help a new generation read the scriptures.

Reason means the way we bring to bear all sorts of human knowledge—scientific, social scientific, philosophical, economic, you name it—on scripture and tradition. It doesn't replace them, but it helps us receive them faithfully in our time. God has given us the gift of intellectual pursuit and deep thought, and we use that gift in discerning the divine will.

Experience… what a loaded word! In discernment, experience doesn't mean any old experience. It's my experience that ice cream is amazing, so ice cream is God. No! Experience refers to experiences of God the Holy Spirit, those moments when the God to whom scripture witnesses touches our lives in all their particularities. Scripture, tradition, and reason help us determine if they are truly experiences of the Living God.

So do we just toss these four in a bag, shake them about, and hope that what emerges is revelation? No! We confess that Jesus is the fullest revelation of the Living God, that scripture witnesses to him in a unique and authoritative way, that tradition helps us engage and read that scripture, that reason helps us critique and appropriate that tradition, and that in our experience we confirm that Living God who reveals herself to us. But don't forget: this is a task for the whole church. We aren't isolated actors who figure all this out on our own. We gather in community to test and encourage each other in our encounters with God. The quadrilateral is a tool of the community rather than the plaything of the individual.

Scripture, then tradition, then reason, then experience. This is how we hear and obey the Word made flesh: God come among God's people to speak and to save. God is speaking! The quadrilateral helps us hear her voice so that we may be doers of her Word.

DAY 4

Fishing for People

> As he walked by the Sea of Galilee, he saw two brothers, Simon, who is called Peter, and Andrew his brother, casting a net into the sea — for they were fishermen. And he said to them, "Follow me, and I will make you fish for people." Immediately they left their nets and followed him.
>
> As he went from there, he saw two other brothers, James son of Zebedee and his brother John, in the boat with their father Zebedee, mending their nets, and he called them. Immediately they left the boat and their father, and followed him.
>
> Matthew 4:18-22

The first time I worked at a summer camp as a teenager, I was more than a little scared and apprehensive. Would I fit in? Would I be accepted? Would there be space for me to find welcome and contribute, or would the staff people be cliquey and territorial and aloof? This camp was the furthest I'd ever been from home for any lengthy duration of time, and I was going in sight unseen, following a recommendation from someone I knew back home.

Upon pulling onto the site, however, my fears were forgotten in all the chaos. We had pulled up just as the camp staff were embarking on their Day-Off Parade. This was a weekly occurrence—I found out—where counsellors, program staff, directors, lifeguards and kitchen staff, all processed to the fried chicken shack down the road, regaled in silly costumes and banging on improvised instruments, for no other reason than their own amusement and that of the lumber truck drivers who rambled down our stretch of Northern Ontario highway. As I stepped out of the car a self-concerned, insecure adolescent, hasty introductions were made, a costume and an overturned bucket was thrust into my hands, and I was swept into the parade of silly servants of Christ who would become, unbeknownst to me, some of the most enduring examples I know of a full, abundant, purposeful, and beautiful life.

I was hooked right from the beginning.

When I read the story of Jesus calling his first disciples, I get a taste of who God is that jives with some of what I experienced in my welcome to camp leadership that day.

I see God as invitational. There is always room for new people to get involved in what God is doing.

I see God as relational. There is a desire to do things together instead of in isolation.

I see God as hopeful. There is a compelling, if ill-defined, trust in the goodness of what lies ahead.

I see God as purposeful. There is an attainable next step on offer, towards that for which we hope.

I see God as creative. There are real-life outcomes connected to God's invitation and our response.

I see God as loving. There is an intimate encounter between God and God's people, where both are seen for who they really are.

I see God as gracious. There is no reason on God's part, apart from God's goodness and love, for why any of this needs to take place.

When you look to Jesus, I pray that you get a taste of who God is and a picture of what God hopes for your life. When you receive a meaningful invitation, I pray you might hear the whisper of God who sees you, and knows you, and longs to be close to you. When you extend a meaningful invitation to someone else, I pray you might feel the presence of God and acknowledge the holy ground on which you stand.

And may you have the courage to leave everything you know and follow Christ, just as the first disciples did, and every disciple has since then.

Questions for Reflection:

Imagine you are one of the fishermen called to leave everything and follow Jesus. What is exciting about that invitation? What is troubling about it?

When have you received a meaningful invitation? When have you extended one? When have you been swept up in a movement of people that seemed to have a life of its own? What might it be like to be swept up in the movement of God's people?

What aspects of God's character make you want to trust God and follow? What questions do you have about God's character that make you hesitate?

What are some of the barriers that prevent people from being drawn into the community of God's people? How might God be calling you to help dismantle those barriers, so that people experience radical welcome and inclusion?

My Daily Discoverment

THE HOPE THAT ALLOWS ME TO STAY
by Alydia Smith

As a Black woman within the United Church of Canada I have had to reconcile my call to love and serve Jesus, with the undeniable harm that the church has caused Black, Indigenous and People of Colour.

There is no denying that the church helped to create the ideological infrastructure of racial hate, and many other forms of systemic oppression, that we are trying so hard to dismantle.

The mainline protestant church in North America is a historic and symbolic White space. Since Europeans started to explore the 'New World' under the Doctrine of Discovery (a Papal edict), the Western Christian's understanding of race has been linked to the need to reconcile the suffering of African descendant people by White Christians of good faith. Every generation expresses this need differently. In my time this has looked like the normalization of harmful stereotypes—particularly those that equate evil, sin, and corruption to Blackness, and the harmful assumption that Black people, countries and communities are in need of 'benevolent aid'.

The church continues to live with this tension. We are trying to deconstruct Anti-Black racism even as we continue to perpetuate hate in our teachings and practices, actions, and reactions. As an unapologetically Black woman, why would I want to associate myself with an institution that celebrates and favours Whiteness at the expense of my Blackness? I have no delusions of grandeur. I do not believe that I can be a voice of lasting change from within the organization, or the proverbial thorn in the side of White Supremacy. Racism within the church is far more complicated than that.

In the end, the resurrected Christ—the fact that the powers and principalities could not kill the Gospel of Jesus—is the hope that allows me to stay within the church. My ancestors, who believed in the words and actions of Jesus of Nazareth, despite the contradictory words and actions of the mainline church, is what has strengthened me for the daily challenge of being a Black body in a White space. I pray that our shared ministry as a church will build on my ancestors' legacy of following the radical, unconventional, and loving way of Jesus above and despite all else.

My Daily Discoverment

MY DISCOVERMENT JOURNEY: WHO IS GOD?

Use this space to journal about any feelings, questions, or discoverments that came to you as you considered the character of God in this section.

www.discoverment.org

Who am I?

Knowing my own belovedness
Days 5 – 8

SET YOUR INTENTION: WHO AM I?

In this second section of reflections, I invite you to consider what it is that God says about who you are. There are so many different things that we could root our identity in—our looks, our abilities, our relationship status, our reputation, etc. What would happen if we rooted our identity in what God says about us? What might open up for us? What might change? What does God say about us, and can we trust it to build our lives upon?

There is a real gift in knowing who you are—how you are wired, what you are good at, what you are passionate about, and how your story intersects with the world around you. Under all those things, however, is the simple fact that you are a beloved child of God. When we dig down deep and set our identity on the foundation of God's love for us, we can start building a life that can withstand all sorts of hardships.

Consider:

- What are some of the pieces that make up my identity as I understand it currently?
- How does my sense of who God is shape my sense of my own identity?
- Is it easy or difficult to receive love from God, from others, from myself? Why might that be?

Let's Pray:

Loving God, thank you for making me who I am. Even though I am still discovering myself and who I might become, I sense that there is something good in me that causes you delight, that I might delight in myself and share with the world around me. Were it not so, I don't believe you would have bothered. Help me discover what love is. Help me to ground my sense of self in your great love for me. Help me to safeguard and hold precious the love you have for all people. Draw me back to your love, when life gets complicated and difficult. I pray in Jesus' name. Amen.

www.discoverment.org

DAY 5

God's Beloved

> In those days Jesus came from Nazareth of Galilee and was baptized by John in the Jordan. And just as he was coming up out of the water, he saw the heavens torn apart and the Spirit descending like a dove on him. And a voice came from heaven, "You are my Son, the Beloved; with you I am well pleased."
>
> Mark 1:9-11

As I write these words, I am sitting at one of hundreds of workstations on the upper level of our university's main library. It is evening and a little quieter than usual on campus, so I actually got one of the workstations that looks out a window—usually these ones are all taken by the time I show up. Through the window in front of me, I can see the lights of other campus buildings, the dark patches that indicate various green spaces on campus, and the steady blinks and flickers of traffic on the main street of our town. And because of the darkness outside, I can also see in that very same window, my own reflection staring back at me, the stacks of books behind me, and the occasional student or professor who walks behind me, burning their own version of the midnight oil.

Jesus is a little like this window before me. When I look to Jesus, I get my best view through to who God is, what God cares about, and how God interacts with the world we live in. Jesus reveals God to me in a way nothing else can.

At the same time, Jesus offers me a reflection back upon myself so I can see who I truly am in God's eyes, who I am at the core of my identity, who I can be apart from all the shame and sin and brokenness and regret that I let gunk up my life. Jesus shows me my true self.

When Jesus was baptized in the Jordan River by his cousin John, a voice came from heaven, declaring, "You are my Son, the Beloved; with you I am well pleased" (Mark 1:11). This voice, according to the Dutch author and spiritual director Henri Nouwen, proclaims this same truth over all of us. Listen to what Henri Nouwen imagines the divine voice saying over you…

> *'I have called you by name, from the very beginning. You are mine and I am yours. You are my Beloved, on you my favour rests. I have folded you in the depths of the earth and knitted you together in your mother's womb. I have carved you in the palms of my hands and hidden you in the shadow of my embrace. I look at you with infinite tenderness and care for you with a care more intimate than that of a mother for her child. I have counted every hair on your head and guided you at every step. Wherever you go, I go with you, and wherever you rest, I keep watch. I will give you food that will satisfy all your hunger and drink that will quench all your thirst. I will not hide my face from you. You know me as your own as I know you as my own. You belong to me. I am your father, your mother, your brother, your sister, your lover, and your spouse… yes, even your child… wherever you are I will be. Nothing will ever separate us. We are one.'* (Nouwen pp. 36-37)

Our belovedness is not something we earn or attain. It is not something we can create for ourselves or receive from the people around us. It is a gift from God. It is the grace of God. It was displayed for us on the cross, and it is proclaimed over us with the rise of each new dawn. It was true about you before you picked up this book, even before you identified with or claimed any kind of Christian identity. It was your truth before you were even born.

So many people spend their whole lives trying to achieve and earn that which is already freely given, and in the meantime, they pour out vast fortunes in time and energy and resources and hopes. God's belovedness and acceptance of us is our starting point in life, not an end goal towards which we strive. Hear that again. God's belovedness and acceptance is our starting point. We're already there. The finish line that so many people believe they must strain to arrive at is actually the starting line. If you get that right, you can be freed up to live a life that really and truly matters.

Beloved ones, as we seek out who we are becoming, may we never forget who we already are. We are the beloved of God. No matter how much you accomplish in life, or how lofty the goals you set for your future, your belovedness is enough to make life meaningful and worthwhile and good. God is well pleased with you already and delights in you as is.

Questions for Reflection:

Who knows you the best? What is the relationship between being known and being loved? What might it say to you that God—who knows you completely, just as you are, warts and all—loves you completely?

In the Nouwen passage, he lifts up a number of things that God proclaims over us as expressions of our belovedness. What affirmations touch you the most? What do you long to hear from God as you think about your future?

So many people do not assume belovedness as a starting point for their relationship with God. Why is this? What might you need to let go of in order to more fully acknowledge yourself as a beloved child of God? Who is someone you know who needs to hear God's affirmation over them? How might you share it?

Who are the models in your life, of people who extend generous, gracious, unconditional love? How might you model your own living after their example? How might receiving and extending God's belovedness look different in your context?

DAY 6

False Voices on Identity

> See what love the Father has given us, that we should be
> called children of God; and that is what we are. The reason
> the world does not know us is that it did not know him.
> Beloved, we are God's children now; what we will be
> has not yet been revealed.
>
> 1 John 3:1-2a

Many of us will remember playing a game, in youth group or some team building session, called Minefield. In it, multiple sets of partners are situated at opposite ends of a room littered with obstacles—squeak toys, mousetraps, plates full of shaving cream, etc. One partner is blindfolded, and the other has to call out instructions to their partner, to help them navigate their way across the minefield. Of course, if you have a critical mass of pairings, the challenge becomes one of distinguishing the voice of your partner from the cacophony of all other voices.

Sometimes life is like a game of Minefield but with steeper consequences than stepping on a squeak toy.

It can be hard to hear God's proclamation of our belovedness over us, in no small part because of all the false voices in our world who will try to drown it out. These voices find all sorts of subtle and pervasive ways to say things like…

You are unworthy of love.
You will never be enough.
You are defined by all your worst mistakes.
You are an abomination.

We hear them from a consumerist society that feeds off our neediness and insecurity. We hear it from other hurting people who attempt to find healing by tearing others down. We hear it faintly in the whispers that try to tell us another story, other than God's truth—like we are what we do, earn, possess, or accomplish. There are lots of people out there who'd be happy to deny us the belovedness God declares over us.

And sometimes we even recognize the false voice as coming from ourselves. Shame echoes within me when I repeat lies about myself to myself. Shame is a belief that I am something bad, right down to my core, which is very different from naming and confronting the less-than-admirable things we all sometimes do. Shame tries to convince me that my true self, all my unique perspectives and gifts, isn't a safe thing to project into the world. So I create all sorts of false versions of myself for public display and consumption.

And strangely enough, shame, and the false versions of myself it creates, can often feel like a comfortable blanket, insulating me from hope and responsibility and other peoples' expectations. Sometimes lies that don't expect too much of me are more comforting than truth that raises up possibility and hope for my future.

When these false voices try to shape our sense of who we are—in ways both overt and subtle—it is important to ground our identities in what God says about us instead. As David Benner writes, an "identity grounded in God would mean that when we think of who we are, the first thing that would come to mind is our status as someone who is deeply loved by God." (Benner, p. 49)

There is something of great value waiting for us, an important call upon our lives, if we can identify and follow God's voice across the minefield of falsehoods that litter our world. But if we can't hear God's voice of truth, proclaiming our identity over us as the beloved, then how can we expect to hear God's voice calling us into tomorrow?

Questions for Reflection:

Life can be noisy and full of voices that pull us in different directions. What are some of the voices filling up the airwaves in your life? In which voices can you hear an echo of God's voice, calling you the beloved? Which voices are telling you something else?

How do you distinguish between shame and other things—like conviction, or guilt, or a holy unrest?

In what ways has shame, or the False Self, been a comfort to you? What might be difficult about letting go of your False Self? What might letting go open up for you?

What might you do to remind yourself of your True Self—being God's beloved child—when life gets noisy?

YOU ARE LOVED. YOU ARE LOVED. YOU ARE LOVED.
by Leanne Friesen

I was 24 years old and working as a youth pastor. I did that job for two and half years in my young twenties, and I truly poured my body and soul into it. I loved it, but it was also exhausting and lonely. I had so much to learn about letting others help me, setting boundaries, and letting myself rest. I felt such a weight, all the time. I was desperate to get everything right, to do just the perfect thing to help my youth, and to please God. I often felt like I was letting God down.

The heaviness of those feelings came over me particularly strongly one Sunday morning during a special youth event. We had a big altar across the front of the church where people could go to pray, and I felt I had to go the altar. I went forward, knelt and prayed. "God," I begged. "Please talk to me. Tell me what to do. Tell me my next steps. I want to get this right."

Over and over I asked God to reveal what I should do next in my ministry, promising to do whatever God asked. I wept over that altar. I was the quintessential image of "pouring my heart out." I so desperately wanted to know what to do.

After a while, I was prayed out and cried out. I wiped my nose and my eyes and went back to my seat. That was when a pastor I knew came over to me.

"Leanne," he said, "Would it be okay if I prayed for you?"

"Sure," I sniffled. (I mean, I'm not one to miss out on a chance for prayer…)

He put a gentle hand on my shoulder, and he prayed something like this: "God, I bring Leanne to you. And I believe you want to say something to her. I believe you want to say to her that you are well pleased with her." There was a bit more, but to be honest I don't remember it. I was completely undone by that simple statement: "You want to tell her that you are well pleased with her."

I had been begging and begging and begging God to speak to me. "Tell me what to do!" I had asked. "Tell me how to live!" And what God wanted to say was: "I'm pleased with you."

"You're already enough."

"You don't have to do anything."

I love you.

Turns out I didn't need any more words or messages—the greatest thing God had to say to me was that I was loved.

I was reminded of this story a while ago when I was with a small group I had been leading. Someone shared how much they wanted to hear from God, that they wanted to know what to do next in their life. I asked if we could pray for them, and they said yes. We gathered around and asked God to speak to this person through us, as we laid hands on their back and listened to see if we felt God saying something for us to pass on. And you know what happened? It shouldn't surprise me.

Person after person said: "The only thing I feel is God telling me to tell you, is that he loves you."

You are loved. You are loved. You are loved.

Here is why I write today. There's a lot out there that may need to be said. But maybe we most need to remember what perhaps doesn't get said enough. You are loved.

Maybe you feel desperate for God to tell you what to do. Maybe you have been pleading for God to give you a message, a sign, a road map. Maybe you are anxious about making the right decisions for school or wondering how to lead your church into the next season or trying to figure out how to make ends meet after losing your job. You are loved.

Maybe you feel lonely, isolated, forgotten. Maybe you don't have a community. Maybe you are disconnected, and, today, it hurts. You are loved.

There are a lot of places where we may want a word from God. But could it be that God's greatest desire for you today is not to tell you what to do, but for you to remember who you are, and whose you are, and that you are, above all, loved?

I think it could be, so just in case let me remind you:

You are loved. You are loved. You are loved.

DAY 7

False Voices on Success

When they came, he looked on Eliab and thought, "Surely the Lord's anointed is now before the Lord." But the Lord said to Samuel, "Do not look on his appearance or on the height of his stature, because I have rejected him; for the Lord does not see as mortals see; they look on the outward appearance, but the Lord looks on the heart."

1 Samuel 16:6-7

"Let the one who boasts, boast in the Lord." For it is not those who commend themselves that are approved, but those whom the Lord commends.

2 Corinthians 10:17-18

If I were to ask you to measure the distance from where you are right now to your place of work or your home or to the moon, you would probably respond with some figure in kilometres or miles or inches or feet. You wouldn't respond in weeks, or kilograms, or volume per square inch.

If I were to ask you how long it's been since your last vacation, you would probably respond with some number of months or years, or decades or hours—not quarts, or thread count, or metric tonnes.

If I were to be rude and ask you your weight, you would probably respond with some number of pounds or kilograms, or with a well-deserved punch to my nose.

Knowing how to measure something correctly, using the right units of measurement, is an important life skill to have. But it's not always easy.

What if I were to ask you if your life has been a success?

Some false voices in our society will tell us that we measure success by things like

- the amount of money we have in our bank accounts
- the number of wins we chalk up in competition
- the amount of prestige we receive from others
- the number of followers we have on social media
- the amount of influence we have over our surroundings
- the number of degrees we earn at school

This picture of success is rampant in academia (think of who gets highlighted in recruitment materials and on posters around campus), business (think of who gets featured in business magazines or investment strategies), popular culture (think of who the hot musicians are right now and what they sing about), and even the church (which is sad). Our fascination with celebrity culture and the cycle of what's hot and what's not, can be attributed to these false notions of success.

Those who follow Jesus have a different model of success to emulate. Jesus, by the criteria listed above, did not lead a very successful life. He was poor, despised, betrayed, and murdered by other more "successful" people of his time.

Success, for those who follow Jesus, is measured more by

- obedience to God
- trust in God
- reliance on God
- faithfulness to God's call
- love for God and God's people

The key difference between these visions of success is that false success draws everything to us, whereas success for the Christ-follower focusses everything on God and the things God loves. There is a pouring out of the self, called kenosis, that is modelled for us in Jesus, which serves as the template for Christian success, if you want to call it that. The self-giving love that we receive from—and see displayed in—Jesus, is an enduring measure of our Christian walk.

The irony is the more we pour out, the more we receive—not in riches or status, but in things like grace, faith, and experiences of the Divine. As Jesus taught, "Those who try to make their life secure will lose it, but those who lose their life will keep it." (Luke 17:33)

Everyone wants to be successful in life. But the way we choose to measure success is one of the key things that shapes our sense of who we might become and what we are called to pursue in our lives.

Questions for Reflection:

There are a lot of false ideas about what success looks like in the world. What are some of the depictions of success touted by the people and institutions in your circles?

Some people will reject Jesus and his teachings because his life wasn't successful enough in their eyes. What would change about Jesus and his message if he were more traditionally successful (rich, powerful, popular, etc.)?

Where, in the life of Jesus, do you see self-giving love modeled for us? Who are the people you know who likewise exhibit this kind of attention towards God and the things God loves? Do you think of them as successful in life?

The idea of self-giving love, or kenosis, can make a lot of people squirm. Is there a limit to how much of the self one ought to give? What does Jesus' example show us? How might you know if you were doing kenosis wrong?

www.discoverment.org

DAY 8

The Wondrous Cross

> For to this you have been called, because Christ also suffered for you, leaving you an example, so that you should follow in his steps... When he was abused, he did not return abuse; when he suffered, he did not threaten; but he entrusted himself to the one who judges justly. He himself bore our sins in his body on the cross, so that, free from sins, we might live for righteousness; by his wounds you have been healed.
>
> 1 Peter 2:21,23-24

When I was a child, I was enamoured with the wonderfully silly and subversive TV show, "Pee-wee's Playhouse." In it, the oddball main character, Pee-wee Herman, entertains and welcomes a wild collection of outrageous and generationally ambiguous friends to his house for playdates and adventures. Characters like Cowboy Curtis, Miss Yvonne, and Captain Carl—as well as a variety of talking robots, furniture and plasticine dinosaurs—all traipsed through the playhouse, and found within it loads of colourful welcome and adventure.

In one episode that particularly stuck with me, Pee-wee is hosting an overnight slumber party and during snack-time reflects dreamily that he loves his fruit salad. His pyjama-clad playmates respond by challenging him to prove it... by marrying it.

With side-eyed bravado, Pee-wee meets their provocation by informing them that he will indeed marry his fruit salad ("Pajama Party" 20:50). The ensuing ceremony is silly, fun, and beautiful—if not legally binding. And it's a good reminder to me and all of us that you can't just say you love someone (or something) if you're not willing to back it up with action.

Proclaiming belovedness over us is no flippant or sentimental remark on the part of the Divine. God backs it up every day, particularly through Jesus' loving action on the cross.

Now, there is a lot going on theologically on the cross, and there are lots of different ways to interpret it. The cross is, after all, the great mystery at the heart of Christian faith. But here are a few affirmations I take from it, that I have built a life upon.

We are God's beloved, in spite of at times being very difficult to love. We all have done things that have strained our relationship with the Divine and have separated us from the source of life, the natural consequences of which is death in its varied forms. Some of these separations are freely chosen and intentional, some are unintentional and unconscious, while others are the results of systems we participate in daily without much thought. We call these particular actions and omissions, and the general condition they create in the world, sin.

We are God's beloved, not because we are perfect and awesome, but because God is. God is so perfect and awesome that, instead of rewriting the rules and turning a blind eye to our sin and its consequences—which would make God a hypocrite and a cheat—God bore the consequences of our sin by enduring death (on the cross) in our place. We call this unmerited goodness towards us grace.

We are God's beloved, not by cheap proclamation but at a cost which we can never repay. In his book *The Cost of Discipleship*, German theologian Dietrich Bonhoeffer makes a distinction between cheap grace—which says everything is okay and easy and hunky dory, even when it's not—and the costly grace offered to us by God, which recognizes, confronts, and calls us to help heal, the real suffering that exists as a result of the sin in the world.

> *Such grace is costly because it calls us to follow, and it is grace because it calls us to follow Jesus Christ. It is costly because it costs a man his life, and it is grace because it gives a man the only true life. It is costly because it condemns sin, and grace because it justifies the sinner. Above all, it is costly because it cost God the life of his Son: 'ye were bought at a price,' and what has cost God much cannot be cheap for us… Grace is costly because it compels a man to submit to the yoke of Christ*

and follow him; it is grace because Jesus says: 'My yoke is easy and my burden is light.' (Bonhoeffer, p. 45)

If Jesus is the Word made flesh, Immanuel, God with us, then his suffering and death is something bigger than the suffering and death of you or me—it is the suffering and death of God's own self. God died on the cross instead of me, bore the consequence of my rejection of the source of life, so that I might have abundant life in all its forms. How can we repay such a gift? What is God's sacrifice worth to us? How am I to respond to this amazing act of grace in my life? We can't respond from a sense of obligation and repayment, but we can respond with love and gratitude, amazement and following ever more expansively Christ's own example. We call this way of living discipleship.

We are God's beloved, called to live a life of resurrection. The story of Jesus and God's loving action among us doesn't end at the cross. God is just getting started with us. There is a piece of God's self-giving love, a share in the death and resurrection of Jesus, that has our name on it. We are called not merely to copy and imitate, but to participate in and renew daily, to reimagine and reapply, God's self-giving love in our time and place, so that new life might flourish in every context. We call this invitation into God's loving work our vocation.

The cross shows us that we are God's beloved, and that our belovedness comes at great cost to our Creator. Let us therefore not treat our belovedness clumsily or neglect it. It was hard won, not by our own accomplishments or standing, but by the perfect sacrifice of Jesus. It is the most precious thing we have, and it is a gift no one can take from us. And though a thousand voices may try to deny it and convince us otherwise, our belovedness is the launchpad from which we step boldly into the future—it is not some goal we are working towards or achievement to be unlocked.

We are the beloved of God, and what we do with our lives is our response to this amazing act of grace.

Questions for Reflection:

Can you remember a time when you experienced love backed up with action? When have you encountered expressions of love that felt cheap or flimsy? What differences did you notice between these two experiences?

How do you understand what is going on at the cross? Why do Christians make such a big deal about it? How might the cross be a launchpad for your considerations about how to live life?

How do you respond to the words sin, grace, discipleship, and vocation? They have served as important anchor points for Christian theology over the centuries. How might they anchor your own considerations about your future?

In the classic hymn "When I Survey the Wondrous Cross" the writer claims that God's love shown on the cross "demands my soul, my life, my all" (Watts). What kind of response does the cross demand from you? In what ways is the cross demanding? In what ways is it a gift? What might it mean for you to give your "all" as a response to God's love?

MY NEW SELF
by Morgan Bell

Go dust off your photo albums and take some time to look through old pictures of yourself. Meander through your Facebook posts from five– maybe even ten– years ago. But be warned! You need to prepare for a rollercoaster of emotions! Laughter—over how you used to look compared to now. Grief—for friends and family no longer with us. Disbelief—at opinions you used to hold or that hairstyle you thought was just so cool (frosted tips, for me). Nostalgia. Surprise. Tears. Smiles.

Why is that? You are the one in those pictures, after all. You wrote those Facebook posts. You wore that unfortunate outfit. Still, for good or for ill, I would bet that those pictures and posts from even a few short years ago show you that—in an important sense—that person is no longer you. You've changed. That "you" from a few years ago is no more.

This exercise is a rough analogy to one of the things Christians confess happened on the cross—our own deaths. The Holy Spirit unites us to Jesus, and "our old self was crucified with him" (Romans 6:6). What is an "old self"? It's that "me" who chooses easy violence instead of difficult peace, self-service instead of worship of God, isolation instead of community, pride instead of humility before God and others. It's the "me" I make myself into, rather than the "me" God created. It's the self you see in the old photograph, the person you can't believe you ever were. And that is precisely the person who dies on Jesus' cross so they might be made alive in his resurrection.

In his birth, Jesus takes on our humanity. He is fully for us, as us. Flesh of our flesh and bone of our bone, Jesus takes our sin and overcomes it. The Spirit unites us to Jesus, so that our "old selves" die on the cross, and so that "new selves" may emerge fresh from the garden tomb by God's power. When you were baptized, you said an "Amen" to this inexhaustible mystery. You acknowledged that not only did Jesus die for you and in your place, but that you died with him – dead to your old self, dead to sin, and made alive to God in Christ Jesus. You are a new creation.

"Fine," you might say. "But, uh… where exactly is this new self?"

If you're anything like me, that "old self" still feels very much alive! I lie and cheat. I'm arrogant and self-serving. I think I know better than everyone else. It certainly feels like that "me" isn't all that old. Scripture, quite cryptically, declares that my new self, my true self, my fully redeemed self, is hid with Christ in God. Enter vocation.

Vocation is the work of discerning who that self is and observing the ways in which the Holy Spirit conforms me to the "me" hid with Christ in God. United with Jesus' death we share in his resurrection life. In discernment, we pray that God shows us who this new risen self is. We pray the Spirit to fashion us into those new selves in Christ. We pray that the work of our lives reveals to others the transformative power of Christ's cross and the new life he bestows on all. We pray that God will continue to stuff our photo albums with evidence of the new life Christ brings.

My Daily Discoverment

MY DISCOVERMENT JOURNEY: WHO AM I?

Use this space to journal about any feelings, questions, or discoverments that came to you as you considered your identity in this section.

_____
_____
_____
_____
_____
_____
_____
_____
_____
_____
_____
_____
_____
_____
_____
_____
_____
_____
_____
_____
_____

www.discoverment.org

What does God do?

Exploring God's work in the world
Days 9 – 12

My Daily Discoverment

✻✻✻✻✻✻✻✻✻✻✻✻✻✻✻✻✻✻✻✻✻✻✻✻✻✻✻✻✻✻✻✻✻

SET YOUR INTENTION: WHAT DOES GOD DO?

In this third section of reflections, I want to invite you to consider God's activity in the world. For some people, there is a certain comfort attached to the idea of God's being, but the idea of God's doing—God's action and activity in our world—opens up a whole new set of questions and complexities. What does God do? How does God do it? Towards what purpose does God act in the world? What do we make of the times when God doesn't act? For many, the idea of an active God is a stretch too far to consider. In many ways, it's easier to believe in a hands-off God that doesn't require too much of us or interfere too much in our lives.

But if we are aiming to discern what we are called to do in the world, should we not at least consider what it is that God is already doing there? Perhaps there might be a hint for the direction our life might take, and a purpose we might take into our hearts.

Consider:

- What do you stand to lose, and what do you stand to gain, by opening yourself to the prospect of an active God in your life? Where have you sensed God's activity in your life so far?
- Where do you currently derive a sense of purpose and direction for your life? How open might you be to a new articulation of purpose? How important is it that your own sense of purpose aligns with God's?

Let's Pray:

Living God, the balance between doing and being is a hard one to maintain. Forgive me when I get that balance wrong. Make me aware of your own being and doing, your character and your activity, in my life, so that I may live a life of wholeness and purpose. Meet with me in these coming days and reveal your loving activity to me. I pray in Christ Jesus. Amen.

www.discoverment.org

****

DAY 9

God's Activity

For the word of God is alive and active. Sharper than any double-edged sword, it penetrates even to dividing soul and spirit, joints and marrow...

Hebrews 4:12a (NIV)

The man went away and told the Jewish leaders that it was Jesus who had made him well. So, because Jesus was doing these things on the Sabbath, the Jewish leaders began to persecute him. In his defense Jesus said to them, "My Father is always at his work to this very day, and I too am working."

John 5:15-17 (NIV)

On February 13, 2019 a group of scientists, educators, and space enthusiasts assembled in NASA's Jet Propulsion Laboratory in Pasadena, California for a sombre and celebratory occasion. They gathered to announce the official end of a Mars rover mission that had launched some 15 years earlier, a mission that surpassed their wildest expectations.

In 2004, two robotic rovers—one named Spirit, the other Opportunity—landed on Mars. The hope was they would spend 90 Martian days collecting data, studying geological compositions, and transmitting images of the Martian landscape back to Earth. Exceeding all hopes, Spirit kept working until 2010. Even better, Opportunity kept at it until June 2018, when a planet-wide dust storm buried its solar panels, and the puppy-sized rover made its last transmission.

Both Spirit and Opportunity had a really good run. The little rovers-that-could broke new ground in terms of Martian exploration. The data they retrieved helped ignite our imagination about inter-planetary exploration, and helped tell the history of – and discover the possibilities that exist on—Mars. When Opportunity went silent and all efforts to reconnect with it had been exhausted, there was a real sense of grief in the scientific community. Grief mixed with celebration. Sometimes life is like that when the ones we love go silent.

There are some who have the impression that God is like a non-functioning Mars rover—far away, silent, lifeless and covered in dust. Maybe God had worked at one point, they tell themselves, for people long ago, but no longer. Maybe God's mission, like that of Spirit and Opportunity, was complete. God might've had a good run, some people attest, but surely that run is now over.

As Christians, we affirm the opposite. We affirm that God is indeed alive and active and intervenes in our everyday world in ways big and small, though not always in the ways or with the timing we expect. We observe a God who reveals to us images of what our world is like and calls us to discover new possibilities of abundant living for all of Creation. Our experience shows us that God does stuff, and that's just as true today as it was in Bible times, as it was before the dawning of Creation. If only we have ears to hear and eyes to see.

Moreover, we affirm that God is active in our world in ways that reveal God's own nature to us. We know God's character, in part at least, by looking at the things God does in our world.

For instance, if you turn to the Psalms, you'll find all sorts of verbs (remember, from back in grade school, those are action words) that indicate the kinds of things God does in the world. Here's a collection of verbs from just one psalm—Psalm 147—that describes the kinds of things God does in the world.

builds up	*casts to the ground*	*satisfies*
gathers	*covers*	*sends*
heals	*supplies*	*spreads*
binds up	*makes grow*	*scatters*
determines	*provides*	*stirs up*
calls	*delights*	*reveals*
sustains	*strengthens*	*satisfies*
	blesses	

When we consider the kinds of actions God undertakes in the world—actions in the list above—we get a sense of who God is. We see God's power, God's goodness, God's love for all Creation, God's love and steadfastness. And when we consider God's most signature action in the world, coming to earth in the form of Jesus, we get a sense of God's longing to be with us in all of our hardship and struggle.

Holy one, grant us the eyes to see, the ears to hear, and the openness of heart to perceive your activity in the world. Help us to know you more, so we may recognize your voice when it calls us.

My Daily Discoverment

Questions for Reflection:

When have you had a sense of God's activity in your own life or the lives of the people around you? What verbs would you attach to God's action as you've known it?

When have you felt a lack of God's activity in your life? What did that stir up within you? Does it feel like absence and neglect, or like freedom and space to breathe? How do you think God views those experiences of distance between us?

When you consider the activity of God as described in scripture, what sense do you get of who God is and what God is like? What is the correlation between action and character in your own life? How else, apart from the actions we engage in, are we known to God and one another?

Psalm 121 describes God as our keeper "who will neither slumber nor sleep". Psalm 139 asks "Where can I go from your spirit? Where can I flee from your presence?" and affirms that God is present to us in all our realities. How might your life be different if you lived each day, expecting and observing God's active presence around you?

DAY 10

The World's Brokenness

> Then I said to them, "You see the trouble we are in, how Jerusalem lies in ruins with its gates burned. Come, let us rebuild the wall of Jerusalem, so that we may no longer suffer disgrace." I told them that the hand of my God had been gracious upon me, and also the words that the king had spoken to me. Then they said, "Let us start building!" So they committed themselves to the common good.
>
> Nehemiah 2:17-18

I remember when my friend Cam broke his arm during high school football practice. It was gross. As he chatted calmly with the volunteer coach about what he should do, his arm dangled at his side. And I seriously thought I would throw up.

I remember when a good friend's parents broke up because of infidelity. I remember losing classmates to overdose, illness, accidents, and suicide. I remember the death of a parent to disease and the emptiness that comes with such a void in one's life.

I remember learning of colleagues in ministry who abused their positions of power, and observing the ripples of harm it caused to the people around them. I remember learning that the church denomination I grew up in, that taught me all about love and nurture and acceptance of diversity, had participated in the Indian Residential School system. This church/government collaboration tore thousands of Indigenous children away from their families in a systemic project of genocide and colonialism.

I remember when friends have been excluded for no other reason than the colour of their skin, gender expression, or who they love. I remember, at numerous times, recognizing and being called out on my own attitudes and assumptions that are rooted in racism, sexism, ableism and homophobia. I remember leaping to attend to my own fragility and discomfort, rather than showing much regard at all for the harm I caused others.

Thinking about all of these encounters with brokenness left me feeling sick to my stomach and wanting to run away. I get nauseous still, when I remember each one of them. And I am embarrassed when I recognize the ways in which I perpetuate, like a song on repeat, the same kind of brokenness in my living today.

Facing the brokenness that exists in the world is an uncomfortable experience, and most of us try to avoid it if at all possible. You don't have to look at too many Instagram accounts to know the pressure we all feel to portray a cheery image, to hide our brokenness away. You don't have to be a member of the richest 1% to know that much of what we take for granted about how the world works is built upon broken relationships, broken promises, broken bodies, and broken systems that perpetrate violence on some people while protecting and nurturing others. There is a lot that isn't right in the world. Generations and generations of brokenness and dysfunction and sin. Many who have the option to hide from it, do.

But when we run away from—or deny—the brokenness that exists around us, we are likely to miss out on much of God's activity in the world. "The LORD is near to the brokenhearted," we are told in Psalm 34:18. If we want to be close to what God is doing in the world, we need to draw near to God in the uncomfortable areas of the world's brokenness—not as fixers or saviours, but as witnesses to both the world's pain and the movement of the Holy Spirit.

God's activity is focussed on the broken places of our world, because God is intent on healing what is broken and restoring what sin has damaged. This determination, this fixation, this project that God is set upon is what theologians call the *missio dei*, or the mission of God.

Dr. Darrell Guder, a missiologist in the Presbyterian tradition, claims that "mission is the result of God's initiative, rooted in God's purposes to restore and heal creation… it is the central biblical theme describing the purpose of God's action in human history." (Guder, 4)

Whenever we feel sent by God to pay attention to the world's pain, to be a healing presence, or to engage in a Spirit-led restorative work—no matter how big or small, global or local—we are engaging in the *missio dei*, God's project of responding to a broken world.

God's response to my own personal brokenness is to send forgiveness and new life through Jesus' death and resurrection.

God's response to our relational brokenness is to send us a model in Jesus, of how to live in a way that expresses God's own self-giving love.

God's response to the world's economic brokenness is to become aligned and embedded with those under the burden of poverty. We sometimes call this alignment and embedding God's preferential option for the poor.

God's response to systemic brokenness is to send us a vision and foretaste of God's reign on Earth, which supersedes and challenges any empire or earthly power. We call this vision and foretaste of what's to come, the Kingdom (or Kin-dom) of God.

And an important part of God's response to the ongoing personal, relational, economic, and systemic brokenness in our world, is to send the church—a rag tag collection of people of faith—to embody wholeness and justice and self-giving love. You and me. The church. In all its glory and splendour and challenges and warts. We are—by God's grace—part of God's response to the world's brokenness.

So grab your antacid tablets, your pink powdery tummy medicine, your herbal tea, and your courage. You might begin to feel a little nauseous. You might weep for sadness. You might see things in yourself and the world around you that you'll wish were not true. But it will be worth it. For if we are to follow God with our lives, we are following God towards the world's brokenness.

www.discoverment.org

Questions for Reflection:

When have you been made aware of the brokenness that exists around you? What did that awareness stir within you? Why is paying attention to the world's brokenness an important first step towards healing? How does unawareness, assumption, and a desire for easy fixes cause the world even further harm?

The biblical story of Nehemiah is one of mending what is broken—in this case, the walls around Jerusalem. Read Nehemiah, chapters 2 and 3. How does God work through the people there to address the brokenness around them? Is it a one-size-fits-all response, or a combined effort that draws on the diversity of everyone involved? How might diverse contributions work to address the brokenness that you see in the world?

My Daily Discoverment

The word "mission" sometimes conjures up pictures of little do-good committees who make presentations at church, or missionaries sent to far off lands to evangelize and colonize. What does the wider language of the missio dei and God's healing activity evoke within you? What kinds of activities do you think could (or could not) be part of God's project to heal the brokenness around us and within us? Might there be room for you—and the things you like doing—in this vision of God's purposeful activity in the world?

Emergency workers are celebrated for their courage because they run towards trouble, when others run away. Reflect on the role courage plays in facing the brokenness that exists within us and our world. When have you displayed courage in your life? Where might you need God to grant you some additional courage as you consider your hopes for the future?

www.discoverment.org

****

HEALING POTENTIAL
by Katie Aitken

I was sick as a child. Not in a tragic way. In usual kid ways, except it happened a lot. Like my parents were on first name basis with ER nurses at our local hospital kind of a lot. I suffered from asthma that literally took my breath away, starting insidiously and becoming worse and worse until I was an exhausted pile on the floor. I would scream in pain with fevers in the night as my ears pressed in pain and eventually ruptured, time after time, despite the surgeries to prevent it—to the point where my classmates at naturopathic medical college were confused looking at my ear drum years later. They brought over the TA who examined me and explained that they were completely scarred.

When I was 12, my parents, I think out of almost desperation, took me to a naturopathic doctor. I was enchanted by her. As my health improved, I first felt my calling specifically towards naturopathic medicine. I had felt the calling before—without a name or a career to guide me—I felt her as a child sitting with plants in the forest. Knowing they had magic in them, in a way all children know things like this, before we teach them to forget.

Naturopathic medicine presented the idea for me that health was more than a physical body, to be plastered over with band-aids when it did not comply with our standards for its productivity. That health and healing were complex. That they came from inside. That the world in itself is infused with healing potential. That both our bodies and this planet seek to be healed as they move towards homeostasis. Just as the skin closes after a cut and reseals itself. Seeds after a fire sprout and begin to grow in the ashes of the forest that was there before. *Vis Medicatrix Naturae*… there is a healing power in nature.

In my clinical work as a naturopathic doctor I treat anxiety and mental health. I see the physical effects the body creates when our existential anxieties are not attended to. When our physical safety is not ensured. When we do not feel we belong. The body holds that for us, and in her desire to keep us safe, in her holy wisdom, she tries to make us aware that something has gone awry. Slowing down the digestive system, raising the blood pressure, robbing the body of human desires for anything from food to sex, screaming "THIS IS NOT OK RIGHT NOW."

And yet underneath all of that…

You are always ok. There is a light in each of us that the darkest depression cannot touch. A peace that cannot be shaken by the strongest uncertainties. The part inside each of us made in the image of God. Our own divinity. The part of you that holds your gifts. The way you show up in the world, not because you are practiced at it but because it comes from your very way of being. Your own giftedness.

If there is one thing I know about anxiety is that living from the place of our own divinity melts it away. When you sit in quiet stillness to discern and then act boldly in congruence with your most authentic self, with your highest hopes and love for yourself and this world, sure—you may feel fear, but you will not be overtaken by it.

Peace be with you.

www.discoverment.org

****

DAY 11

God's Kingdom. Already and not yet.

"Our Father in heaven, hallowed be your name.

Your kingdom come. Your will be done, on earth as it is in heaven."

Matthew 6:9b-10

The old, classic movie *Stand By Me* is a nostalgic story of four teenagers on a journey, and embedded within it is possibly the grossest tale—told by one of the characters—of a pie-eating contest / vomit spectacle. *The Princess Bride*, for all its fairytale heroics and meme-worthy quotes, is bracketed by the over-arching story of a sick boy and his grandfather. Many of our great stories—from *Arabian Nights*, to *The Lord of the Rings*, and even the Gospel accounts of Jesus—have embedded within them smaller narratives that help enliven, fill out, and give new perspective to the overall story.

Like these great works of art, your life is a story embedded within a much larger story of God's relationship with Creation. It's a story we can trace through the narrative arc of scripture.

The Biblical narrative begins, in the book of Genesis, with a story of wholeness and tranquility. In it, the Creator walks and talks with the Creation, death and shame are yet unknown, there is equality between men and women, and every need is provided for. The story of the Garden of Eden is a picture of wholeness and wellbeing that we can only imagine.

The Biblical narrative ends, in the book of Revelation, with a mirror image of wholeness, where things are once again put to right, and death and shame are once more powerless over us. In depictions of the established reign of Christ, there is again unity of purpose and mind between diverse peoples, with everyone gathered around the heavenly throne. The fulfillment of the Kingdom of God is a heavenly future that, like Eden, I can only imagine and anticipate.

Everything between these two images of wholeness—including most of the Bible's stories, the history of the church, and the times in which we live—is another story completely. We are in the deep valley, where peril and dangers abide. Things here are messy and tragic and hard. Life here is stained by the consequences of brokenness and sin.

In the late 1980s, the famous folk-singer Bob Dylan went through a period where his music expressed a particular type of Christian devotion. In this period, he wrote a song called "Everything is Broken." Look it up if you get the chance—it's kind of funky and folksy and fun. In it, an older comeback Dylan sings about broken bottles and plates, broken heads and vows, broken hearts and treaties. There's no good denying it, the song tells us. It's useless to hide away. Everything is broken.

Living as we do, in between the wholeness of Eden and the promise of heaven, it can be easy to believe, like Dylan expresses, that everything indeed is broken. But that's not entirely true, is it? For even though there is brokenness all around us and sin touches even the very ways we perceive things, we still get glimpses of goodness and wholeness and justice and peace that poke up out of the rubble every once in a while.

Ours is a brokenness to which we aren't abandoned, a brokenness in which God remains active, a brokenness where God still shows up. The story of this in-between time is full of competing wills and agendas and voices, many of which seem to run counter to God's purpose and hopes for our lives. But if we listen, we can hear God's call through all the clatter. If we are attentive, we can experience a little piece of God's reign, right now in our everyday lives.

The Kingdom of God is the metaphor that scripture uses to describe the settings where God's purpose for our lives is realized, where God's hopes for us bloom into being, and where the divine authority is given precedence over all other contenders. It borrows and subverts the language of empire; God's "kingdom" is not coercive or manipulative or power-wielding over others. Instead, it is invitational, participatory and spiritual—like no other kingdom on earth. In some contexts, people use the language of God's kin-dom, or the beloved community to emphasize that God's purpose and hopes for our world are relational, like a diverse human family or neighbourhood that shares goodness and trust with one another.

Jesus spoke about the Kingdom of God as something that grows, like a mustard seed (Matthew 13:31), or some yeast amongst a batch of doughy bread (Matthew 13:33).

Jesus spoke about the Kingdom of God as something that is worth giving everything to obtain, like a valuable pearl (Matthew 13:45) or buried treasure (Matthew 13:44).

Jesus spoke about the Kingdom of God as something that wasn't far off and distant, but is so close it is actually among you in your brokenness. It is like the good wheat that grows up through the weeds that a saboteur had sewn in your field (Matthew 13:24-30).

We get a glimpse of the Kingdom of God when the powerless and marginalized find their voice and gain agency. We see it when we receive or extend an act of loving kindness or compassion. We see it when we gather in community to sing praise to God and to meditate on God's promises. We see it when we remember, retell, and relive the stories of God's loving action among us in our broken and messy world.

The Kingdom of God is among us, like a loot bag that reminds us of a birthday party from our youth.

The Kingdom of God is among us, like a familiar voice we hear across a crowded room.

The Kingdom of God is among us, like the hors d'oeuvres of a banquet that is still being prepared.

Not everything is broken. The Kingdom of God is already here and not yet fully realized. We live with one foot in the brokenness of this world, and another in the wholeness and splendour of heaven. And we get to choose from which foot we will leap into our future.

Perhaps we can use the glimpses we receive of the Kingdom of God to guide us towards the kind of future God has in store for us. Perhaps we can live in a way that serves as a window to the kin-dom of God for someone else. Perhaps God might work through us and with us to establish God's beloved community a little more fully, here on earth. Perhaps we have a part in the story God is writing.

My Daily Discoverment

Questions for Reflection:

Take a look at the story of Eden (Genesis 1 and 2) and the vision of the fullness of God's kingdom expressed by John of Patmos in the book of Revelation (try chapters 4, 7, 21 and 22). How are they similar? How are they different? What do they both tell you about God's picture of wholeness?

How might a wide view of scripture—as a story from wholeness through brokenness to a new kind of wholeness—influence your reading and application of the Bible? How might it give context to individual stories or reframe traditional "clobber passages" that are used to harm people?

A paradox is when two seemingly incongruous things are true at the same time. The paradox of the Kingdom of God is that it is both already with us and not yet fully realized. It is both near and far. How comfortable are you with paradox? What other paradoxes can you see at play in the Christian life? What role might paradox play as you contemplate your future?

Sometimes churches suggest that it is our responsibility to build the Kingdom of God or extend it through our own efforts, work, and striving. The Bible though, doesn't emphasize that. Rather, the Kingdom of God is most often portrayed as something we receive, notice, or enter. What does it free up in you to think of the Kingdom of God as something God initiates, instead of us initiating? How might you orient your sense of vocational calling, to receive, notice, and enter the Kingdom of God every day, even as you participate in it?

DAY 12

Partners With God

> His divine power has given us everything we need for a godly life through our knowledge of him who called us by his own glory and goodness. Through these he has given us his very great and precious promises, so that through them you may participate in the divine nature.
>
> 2 Peter 1:3-4a (NIV)

When I was young, my bedroom would get so messy, it would be difficult to find things. Sometimes it would be so gross that foul odours would rise up from Lord knows where. Sometimes the state of my room became an occasion for sharp words between my parents and I. And on rare occasions, when it became too much for my poor mother to bear, sometimes I would come home and find my room had been magically cleaned and reordered for me. More often, however, my mother would corner me and *invite* me to spend a Saturday morning cleaning my room under her supervision.

When my mother would clean my room for me, I would feel a bit of shame because I knew my laziness had caused her to take time from her day. I would feel a bit out of the loop because she would organize my stuff differently than I would have. I might even feel a little worried that she might stumble upon some personal items that I wanted to keep private.

When my mother would clean my room with me, it was a lot more work, it was a little bit awkward, but there would be some laughs, some lessons, and some time well spent together along the way.

In both cases, I ended up with fresh sheets, a clean floor, and an ordered room in which to flop around. But in working with my mom, instead of against her, I gained an awful lot more than just the end result.

There is a big difference between doing something *for* someone, and doing something *with* someone.

God is determined to mend and heal the brokenness in our world. God is willing to take an active role in fulfilling this vision of wholeness and healing. But God's design, God's preference, God's invitation, is to work with us in the healing of Creation. God wants to mend the brokenness of our world *with* us, not *for* us.

The work of providing justice for the oppressed and healing for the brokenhearted is not God's work alone, it's ours as well. In the same way that God has sent Jesus to the world to be an agent of peace and hope and reconciliation and love, so too are we sent into the world to engage in our own piece of God's redeeming work.

But we are more than just partners and co-creators with God—we are friends of God as well.

Do you remember when your teacher would assign lab partners or designate work groups for a class assignment? Didn't you always hope you would be paired with your friend? In John 15:15, Jesus says, "I no longer call you servants, because a servant does not know his master's business. Instead, I have called you friends, for everything that I learned from my Father I have made known to you." We are partners and co-creators with God, we are invited into the work God is doing, but our partnership is not coercive or awkward. Instead, it is marked with real friendship. It is a joy to be working with our friend. Friends trust one another with things that are important.

Our vocation is God's invitation to be partners in the important work set aside for us. Will you grab hold of your share in God's important work in the world? Will you work alongside God in establishing a fairer, more beautiful, more life-sustaining world? Can you think of a more worthy project to give your life to, or anyone you would rather have by your side?

Questions for Reflection:

The term "mission" derives from the language of being sent. Sometimes we also use the image of an invitation to participate in God's work. How is being sent different from being invited? Which one resonates most with your sense of God's call upon your life right now? Is there a time when you can imagine needing to lean on another image or word to describe your sense of vocational call?

Are you somebody who likes to work independently or in a partnership? How might being a co-creator with God affirm or challenge your usual patterns of work and creativity?

Some people will affirm that it's not the process or the collaboration that matters, but rather it's the results that are really important. If God were only interested in results, how different would our relationship with the Divine look?

Does God really need us for the completion of God's work? How might your answer shape your understanding of your relationship with God?

My Daily Discoverment

✲✲✲✲✲✲✲✲✲✲✲✲✲✲✲✲✲✲✲✲✲✲✲✲✲✲✲✲✲✲✲✲

ABUNDANT LIFE FOR ALL
by Mitchell Anderson

I'm sometimes asked why I chose to be a minister, and I always laugh and say I never would've chosen to do this. I'd be making a lot more money as a corporate lawyer or banker or something equally lucrative. But God who is endlessly creative and redemptive and sometimes mischievous had different plans for me than I might have had for myself, and my life is all the richer for it.

Paul advised his friends in Corinth to imitate him as he sought to imitate Christ (1 Cor. 11:1). Paul challenged his friends in Philippi to have the same mind as Christ (Phil. 2:5) as they lived out the way of Jesus together. As followers of Jesus, our lives are meant to be changed. More and more our lives take the shape of Christ's life. We are in Christ, and through Christ we participate in the mission of God. This is what theologian Michael Gorman calls "missional theosis"—by participation in the mission of God for the renewal of the world our own lives are changed to be more like Christ (Gorman, xvii). This should extend to our vocational lives as well. As we follow Jesus who is sent into the world for wholeness, healing, and justice, we ourselves become more and more people of wholeness, healing, and justice.

Jesus came that all might have abundant life (John 10:10), and we can see this in all of Jesus' ministry. How then can our vocations contribute to God's mission of abundant life? Jesus heals the sick, joins in solidarity with the outcast and excluded, and challenges oppressive systems. Like Jesus we too can heal—healing bodies, hearts, minds, and spirits. We can also heal broken and wounded societies and relationships. We can bring joy and delight in acts of care and joy, in art and wonder. Similarly, we can also tackle the underlying conditions that prevent people from experiencing abundant life by working for just and inclusive societies. Each of us in our own way can help one another experience abundant life, and in seeking God's abundant life we find that our own lives abound in grace more and more. For me my calling and vocation have invited me to experience kinds of abundance I could never have imagined, supporting people in challenging times, accompanying people hurting, and in so many ways trying my best to help people know that God's grace and love are with them each and every day.

While God desires abundant life for us, we must be careful not to imagine then that God's abundance looks like our abundance. We are sometimes tempted to imagine that abundant life looks like the things we think we want: money, status, power, privilege, all the things the world tells us are a good life. Jesus' ministry, however, is one of sacrifice and self-offering, leading to him dying for us, even while we were sinners (Rom. 5:8). In the same way, Jesus invites us to be willing to die for one another as the greatest act of love (John 15:13), teaching that whoever grasps onto their own life will lose it, but whoever gives their life away will find it (Luke 17:33). Our vocations, then, should have at their very heart a sense of sacrifice, a commitment to the other. Yes, we might find some status or prestige along the way from our vocational life, but our core motivation should be about service, a willingness to sacrifice, seeking the well-being of others and not ourselves. I know for myself my calling to be a minister has required sacrifice—personal, professional, and financial—in order to serve where I believe God wants me. By many standards I've given up a lot, but there is something incomparably joyful about doing what the Creator of the universe wants you to do. Many of the most true and beautiful and good things in life can ever happen through some kind of sacrifice, saying no to some things we want so we can say yes to what God wants.

Just as Jesus' mission is to offer himself to give abundant life to all, so too he invites us to offer ourselves to give abundant life to all. In joining Jesus in this mission, we find our lives are changed, not always in ways we expect or might have chosen for ourselves. We find our lives are their most abundant right when we most give our life away for the sake of the world.

My Daily Discoverment

MY DISCOVERMENT JOURNEY: WHAT DOES GOD DO?

Use this space to journal about any feelings, questions, or discoverments that came to you as you considered the activity of God in this section.

_____
_____
_____
_____
_____
_____
_____
_____
_____
_____
_____
_____
_____
_____
_____
_____
_____
_____
_____
_____
_____
_____

www.discoverment.org

What am I called to do?

Listening for my vocational call
Days 13 – 27

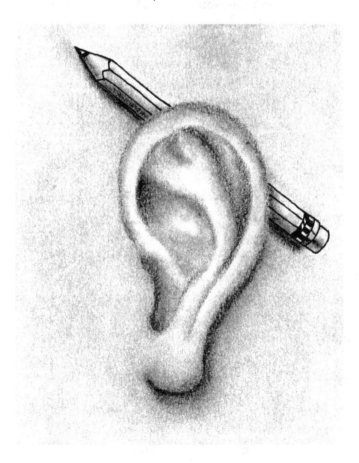

My Daily Discoverment

✶✶✶✶✶✶✶✶✶✶✶✶✶✶✶✶✶✶✶✶✶✶✶✶✶✶✶✶✶✶✶✶

SET YOUR INTENTION: WHAT AM I CALLED TO DO?

In this fourth section of reflections, I want to invite you to consider the contours of your vocation. What does it mean to participate in God's healing work in the world? What part of that work is yours, and what is meant for someone else? How has God equipped you and situated you for a lifetime of meaningful work—both within and beyond your prospective employment? What will this work require of you? Will there be any room left for joy and fun, or is vocation all serious business?

There is lots to consider, so you'll notice this is one of the lengthier sections in this workbook. Hopefully—having considered God's character, your own belovedness, and the kind of work God is doing in the world—you feel prepared to consider your own calling and vocation as it beckons you towards your future.

Consider:

- What do you hope to get out of your life? What is open for negotiation? What isn't?
- What inklings have you had so far about what kind of life or work you are meant for? What has informed that sense of yours? What pressures are attached to a developing sense of purpose?
- How do you feel about the idea that God knows you completely and has equipped you for something? What do you find helpful or comforting when you are uncertain about the direction of your life?

Let's Pray:

Creator God—you are love, you give love, and you invite me into meaningful participation in your loving work in this world. Help me to hear your loving voice calling my name. Permit me to see myself and the world as we truly are. Give me the imagination to see the world and my life unfolding in new ways, empowered by your Spirit. Take my life and create something beautiful with it. Amen.

www.discoverment.org

****

DAY 13

Listening for God's Voice

My sheep listen to my voice; I know them,
and they follow me.

John 10:27 (NIV)

When my wife was pregnant with our children, I would skooch down on our bed so my head rested on her belly, and we would read stories to our children, so they would begin knowing the voice of their parents who loved them.

When I am driving in my car and CBC Radio rebroadcasts a warm familiar voice, like Sheilagh Rogers or Stuart McLean or anyone on the Royal Canadian Air Farce, I am transported back to memories of my childhood—washing with my parents in the kitchen of my childhood home, or eating lunch after church on a quiet Sunday afternoon.

When I hear a really good preacher proclaiming the word of God with power, using all the resources of volume, cadence, conviction and tone, I feel like I am before a door that stands open to the very presence and truth of the Divine. I am in touch, through the power of their voice, with a truth that feels both mysterious and familiar at the same time.

So much is conveyed and held in one's voice—warmth, security, affirmation, and intimacy—qualities that communicate their own truth, quite separate from the content of what is being conveyed.

The term vocation comes from the Latin word 'vocare' or voice. When you go for vocal lessons, you are being trained to use your voice; it's the same root word for vocation. So when we begin thinking about vocation, we don't actually begin by discerning the content of God's invitation. Rather we begin by building a familiarity with the voice of God—knowing its richness, its warmth and its tone, and growing more confident in it day by day.

Dallas Willard, in his book Hearing God, says, "It is much more important to cultivate the quiet, inward space of a constant listening than to always be approaching God for specific direction" (Willard, p. 262). Isn't it lovely to imagine God's warm rich tone of friendship speaking constant words of affirmation and care over you? It's there, if we might only open ourselves to listen.

One of the ways we grow familiar with the quality of God's voice is through consistent and imaginative engagement with spiritual practices.

You are likely familiar with a handful of different spiritual practices. According to Richard Foster, some are inward (things like meditation, prayer, fasting, study), some are outward (things like simplicity, solitude, submission, service), others are corporate (things like confession, worship, guidance, celebration). Our Christian tradition is full of spiritual practices. There are books and websites galore, promoting the newest, the oldest, the most obscure, and the most trendy spiritual disciplines, exercises and regimes. It can all be quite dizzying and confusing. And sometimes we can approach the vast buffet of spiritual practices with the wrong impressions, understandings, and motivations.

Spiritual practices are not solely about receiving messages or direction from God; they are about forming our heart's capacity to hear God's voice and sense God's presence.

Spiritual practices are not about impressing God with our piety, efforts, and steadfastness; they are about opening ourselves to be more aware of and reliant on God's grace and goodness.

Spiritual practices are not about expressing the right denominational or religious identity; they are about nurturing your relationship with God and coming into God's presence with your whole truth—the good, the bad, and the ugly parts of it.

Spiritual practices are not some kind of mystical hokey pokey, TikTok dance, or video game cheat code that will gain you access to the secrets of the world; they form us, over the course of a lifetime, into who we are becoming. They remind us of who God says we already are.

Spiritual practices make the most sense in the context of a loving friendship with God. Think of them as ways by which you listen to and converse with your friend. What kinds of things do you like to do with your friends—hike? text? eat? go on adventures? Maybe there's a clue there, pointing towards a spiritual practice that might develop your friendship with God.

If your spiritual practice routine is feeling a little clunky, dry, or stale; if it's hard to hear the quality of God's voice; or if your practice misrepresents the divine voice speaking to you, change it up and try something new. If your spiritual practice routine makes you feel like a failure or induces shame in you, step away and try a new approach. If your spiritual practice routine is too easy and familiar, and the image it gives you of God is too small, try something different that will form in you a capacity to hear God's voice anew in your life.

If we are to respond to God's invitation in our life, we need to be able to hear God's voice rightly—in all its depth, warmth, graciousness, and love.

My Daily Discovermen

Questions for Reflection:

What has your experience of spiritual practices been? What is a practice that has been helpful for you in the past? What is a practice that you have let go of? What is a new practice that you are interested to explore and experiment with?

Sometimes we get the impression that only spiritual giants—like pastors or wise elders or published theologians or bloggers—engage in spiritual practices, and that if we don't experience revelation and fireworks and angelic choirs every time we pray, we're not doing it right. The reality is, engaging a spiritual practice takes practice. It is not always rewarding or extraordinary. It sometimes feels like work. When have you let your expectations, caricatures, or comparisons keep you from engaging a spiritual practice? What might it look like to get better at the spiritual life?

Spiritual practices are sometimes called spiritual disciplines. What does the language of disciplines bring to your mind? What is helpful or unhelpful about the language of spiritual disciplines?

Brother Lawrence was a French Roman Catholic monk of the 17th century. He famously wrote about his practice of attuning himself to the presence of God in the simplest of activities, like washing the dishes. Brother Lawrence reminds us that any task can be a spiritual practice, what matters most is the intention with which we engage it. What is an everyday task that you do already that you might transform into a spiritual practice by applying a new intention? What structure or patterns might you develop to help draw your attention to God's presence in that task, rather than letting the moment slip away?

DAY 14

Vocation vs. Call

> While they were worshiping the Lord and fasting, the Holy Spirit said, "Set apart for me Barnabas and Saul for the work to which I have called them." Then after fasting and praying they laid their hands on them and sent them off.
>
> Acts 13:2-3

The terms *vocation* and *call* both stem from the idea of listening for the voice of God. Vocation, you'll remember, comes from the Latin word "vocare" which means voice. The idea of one's call presumes there is someone using their voice, and there is something important to communicate, something to listen for, something to receive. Whether you're making a phone call, a moose call, or a call to action, the idea is that you are using your voice. There's something important to be heard.

Because of their similar roots, the terms vocation and call sometimes get used interchangeably in the church. But I've come to think of them slightly differently, and in doing so, have found a helpful framework for listening to God in my life. Ultimately, it might not matter what labels you use, so long as you get the differences clear. But here's how I've come to think of the differences between call and vocation.

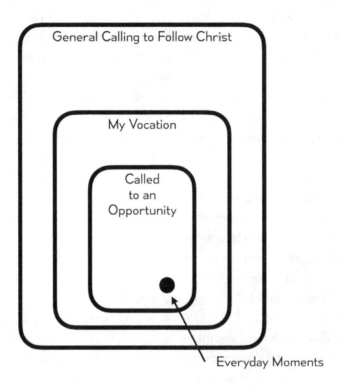

First of all we receive our general calling to follow Christ. We can read all about these kinds of call stories in the Gospels, where simple fishermen, tax collectors, revolutionary zealots, and a wide array of diverse people drop everything they have and follow Jesus. Perhaps you have your own version of this story in your life, where you've found something compelling about the person and teachings of Jesus, and have decided to follow him, even if you're not exactly sure what that entails. Baptism (and its capstone experience in some traditions, called Confirmation) is a moment where we step into this general calling, to live and learn and grow in the Way of Jesus. It's the calling of a lifetime, it takes precedence over all other calls, and though we may discern and respond to a thousand twists and turns within in, this general calling has framed the lives of Christians over the centuries. I may not know where my life will lead me, but I pray it may always be rooted in my desire to follow Jesus.

Secondly, within that general calling, we discern our vocation. Our vocation is an area of work and participation in God's project (*missio dei*), that we feel equipped for and drawn towards by God. Vocation sets us apart. Where our general calling to follow Christ unites us with other Christians, our vocation recognizes that we are equipped differently, positioned differently, and tasked with different parts of God's healing work. One vocation is not better than another, or more important. They're just different. Your vocation may be different than mine, and that's okay for both of us.

The American novelist and theologian Frederick Buechner describes our vocation as "the place where your deep gladness and the world's deep hunger meet" (Buechner, p. 119). There is an element of personal joy in one's vocation (feeling equipped, passionate, gifted in, suited for, and fed by the work of your vocation), as well as a recognition of the need for it—an inherent healing of some aspect of the world's brokenness within it.

When listening for your vocation, I've found it important to resist getting too specific. I like to think of my vocation as being a field of play that God has invited me into—my vocation gets me to the right ballpark, for the next steps of my discernment. For instance, I identify the spiritual care of young people as my vocation. I've found there is much need in this location, and I feel equipped for it via my passion, gifts, etc., but within that vocation, there is still lots of wiggle room to figure out the specifics. You might hear God's voice leading you to a vocation in teaching, or health-care, or business, or hospitality, or environmental conservation, or ministry... or any number of other settings that combine your own gladness and the world's need. You might begin shaping a sense of your vocation when you consider your gifts, what classes you enjoy, when you receive encouragement and praise from others, or when you feel yourself coming alive and engaging certain issues, communities or activities.

There is often something daunting about one's vocation. The work God assigns you will likely outlast your contributions to it. The scope of your vocation should be big enough to become your life's work; if you solve it in your lifetime, you likely set your sights too low. Sometimes your sense of vocation will evolve over time, but probably less dramatically than some other aspects of your life.

And there is something paradoxical about a vocation. Your vocation will be a source of great joy and discontent at the same time. It will stir your creativity and keep you awake at night. In describing vocation, Buechner adds, "Neither the hair shirt nor soft berth will do" (Buechner, p. 119). Your vocation is not meant to be entirely comfortable and easy, nor a source of constant lament. There will be challenging and joyful things about it, often simultaneously. Sometimes we describe our vocation as the work we simply "must" do, whether you're paid for it or not. Your vocation is the unresolved, overwhelming, paradoxical, and compelling, area of work you were made for.

Once we've identified a broad vocational area, we then seek to discern a call to a specific opportunity, a particular context in which you can live out your vocation. Some church traditions have a wonderful practice when hiring a new minister. They invite candidates to lead worship with their prospective congregation one Sunday. Instead of calling it an audition, they call it "preaching for a call." The idea is to test the fit, to see if the candidate and the congregation can both affirm that God is calling this person to this specific ministry. Nobody is questioning whether or not the candidate is suitable for ministry in general; instead they're discerning if this is the right opportunity for this person right now.

Over the course of your life, specific opportunities will come and go. Some, you will feel excited about—others, less so. Some opportunities work out for a while, and then run their course. Other opportunities will open up new insights and will help you articulate things about yourself, the world, and your vocation that you didn't know going in. In some cases, the opportunity will align with your needs for employment and a career. Other times, it won't, and instead you'll find the right opportunity in your relationships with others, in your volunteer work, etc. Sometimes you'll approach an opportunity with a measure of freedom and choice. Other times, the opportunity will feel a bit more restrictive, like a duty or obligation. Sometimes it may feel like there are more opportunities than you know what to do with. Other times, it may feel like a long time in the wilderness between anything that even remotely resembles an opportunity to live into your vocation.

My Daily Discoverment

When I am rooted in my general calling to follow Christ, and I am confident of the vocational field for which I'm equipped, I find I can withstand the ebbs and flows of different opportunities as they come and go. My life becomes less defined by my opportunities, and I am better prepared to embody the character of God in the everyday moments that present themselves to me. It is, after all, the everyday moments—where I can choose to embody grace and love, or stay mired in crabbiness and self-interest—that make up my life, and ultimately serve to bring healing (or destruction) into the world. It doesn't matter a hill of beans what I think about my vocation or where I identify my call if it doesn't lead me to actually be good to my neighbour or gentle with Creation in the everyday moments of my life.

www.discoverment.org

Questions for Reflection:

When have you encountered the terms "vocation" and "call" before? Do you think of them as being similar or different? How so?

Consider Frederick Buechner's description of vocation as the intersection your own "deep gladness" with the world's "deep hunger." How do you distinguish your deep gladness from a mere whim or self-interest? How do you distinguish the world's deep hunger from its superficial demands? What helps you stay focussed on the depths of your personal and societal experiences? What happens when your considerations run too shallow?

My Daily Discoverment

What is the work that you simply must do? Can you identify it and put language to it or is it too early? Are there any hints, stirrings, or wonderings that might eventually form into a sense of vocation for you? Do you approach these questions with a sense of urgency and pressure, or is there some spaciousness and playfulness to your vocational listening? Can it be both?

In what ways does the call to a specific opportunity feel different from the general calling to follow Christ? In what ways is it similar?

www.discoverment.org

****

DAY 15

Knowing Yourself and the World

> For we are what he has made us, created in Christ Jesus
> for good works, which God prepared beforehand
> to be our way of life.
>
> Ephesians 2:10

Every September, our university hosts Orientation Week as a way to welcome first year students to campus. It's a week full of learning events, campus tours, social connecting, and freebies—free food, free concerts, free swag of all sorts. There can be a lot of pressure on incoming students during O-Week to find new friends, find their way, and find what the university experience is going to be like for them.

It can also feel like a week full of small talk. Where are you from? What are you studying? Are you living in residence? There's only so much you can ask a complete stranger, hoping that some commonality or interesting factoid will jump out and spark a deeper, more meaningful conversation. Sometimes well-meaning residence staff, student government officials, or chaplains run silly get-to-know-you games where we determine who's a cat person and who's a dog person, who's an early riser and who's a night owl, etc. These goofy identifiers are never really the point of the exercise. The hope is always that something will spark a further conversation, a doorway will open up and lead towards personal sharing, deeper relationship and community-building.

Some people love Orientation Week. Others see it as something to endure. But if you're going to make connections at university (or elsewhere in life) small steps like get-to-know-you games are important building blocks to take you somewhere deeper.

As we seek to connect with our vocation—the broad area where our deep gladness intersects with the world's deep hunger—it can feel like a bit of a get-to-know you game. There are two things our vocation requires us to know deeply, where superficial knowledge will not do: ourselves and the world.

We get to know ourselves deeply by exploring how we are wired by our Maker and gifted by the Spirit. There are loads of tools such as the Enneagram, Myers-Briggs style personality tests, and various spiritual gift surveys, that can help build self-awareness in these areas. Forget those Internet quizzes that tell you which cartoon princess you are or what *Friends* character you're most likely to date—there are better tools out there. As we mature, we become aware of the things that we're good at, the various charisms or gifts by which the Spirit equips us. We begin to identify what we are passionate about and what makes us come alive through various practices like journalling, contemplation, and discussing with a mentor or friend. Hopefully these explorations also lead us towards deeper self-reflection, where we can acknowledge and take ownership of tender things such as our traumas, our stories, our social locations, and our blind spots. Knowing yourself deeply is important work for those seeking to identify their vocation.

Likewise, we get to know the world deeply by engaging in experiential learning. Don't just think about the world. Get out in the world and experience it! Push beyond your comfort zone and try new things. Volunteer. Go on an exchange. Ask your crush out on a date. Then reflect on your experiences—ask good questions, discuss your experiences with people you trust, pray about what happened and how your felt about it. Formulate some assertions based on your experiences, about the world that you live in and how it works. Where is it broken? What feels like wholeness? Hold your assertions loosely and test them out. Refine them and make your assertions better. Seek new experiences and try it all again. Hopefully by living into this experiential learning spiral, you'll be empowered to see through the oceans of misinformation that exist in our world. At the very least, you'll have come to your knowledge of the world through real lived experience, not what someone else has told you. You'll be able to distinguish some truth in the world, and think beyond yourself so you can align your perspective with others, particularly the marginalized and oppressed, whom you will know by name. Knowing the world deeply, from your own lived experience, is important work for those seeking to identify their vocation as well.

We will never know ourselves or the world completely. Paul reminds us that we see both as if looking through a mirror, dimly (1 Corinthians 13:12). There is some humility required of those who are seeking their vocation and the work to which they are called.

But just as God has been revealed to us in Jesus, so too can we ask God to reveal our true selves and some truth about the world we live in. We may never know ourselves or the world completely, but with God's help we can know enough to love them both, even if imperfectly.

And when we and the world feel unknowable and unlovable, we can rest in God's perfect love for both. Sometimes that's a good enough place to start.

Questions for Reflection:

How do you feel about small talk? What are your favourite topics for small talk or ways of getting to know new people? What is the difference between knowing someone deeply and knowing them only superficially? What does it look like to know the world deeply, rather than merely on the surface?

What is something you are learning about yourself these days? What about yourself are you still hoping to explore? What tools might be helpful in your own self-exploration?

What are some of the more formative experiences in your life? What assertions did you make about the world or yourself because of them? How have your assertions been refined over time?

Why is it important to remain humble about our self-awareness and understandings of the world? How might God's perfect knowledge and perfect love be a starting point for your considerations of vocation?

My Daily Discoverment

✳✳✳✳✳✳✳✳✳✳✳✳✳✳✳✳✳✳✳✳✳✳✳✳✳✳✳✳✳✳✳

ASKING BETTER QUESTIONS
by Cameron Fraser

The meeting closed, and I thought to myself, immediately, that I wanted to quit. ASAP!

But when I had a chance to pause, attend to my feeling of discouragement and disconnection, I was able to ask myself, what was it about this particular meeting?

Was it that I felt unable to be the version of myself I want to be?

Was it the negative patterns of interaction?

Eventually these questions, and sitting with the emotions they provoked within me, helped me understand what it was about the particular meeting that left me feeling so discouraged, and I was able to bring a suggestion for a new way of decision-making and continue to participate in work that I believed in strongly.

The Daily Examen is a practice rooted in Ignatian (aka Jesuit) Spirituality that honours emotions as a source of insight. The Examen encourages me to take seriously that I am an emotional being and that my emotions are not a barrier to decision-making.

As the name suggests, the Examen is best practiced regularly—daily even—pausing and offering curious and compassionate attention to moments of consolation and connection, of desolation and disconnection.

For me, I take some time in the evening to think back, slowly, over what happened in my day. I think about the things I did, my interactions with others, the things I thought about, and I seek to bring to focus how I was feeling, or how I feel looking back.

Doing this in a comfortable, safe space gives me the space to be aware and attentive without missing out the beautiful stuff the feeling of deep satisfaction and enjoyment while also not feeling overwhelmed in the moment by the harder, junky feelings.

This allows me to ask better questions.

"Should I quit or continue?" which is a limiting binary, becomes richer and, in my opinion, more helpful.

Asking "what is it about this work/task/group that has me feeling discouraged?" allows me to more clearly name what I value, what excites and motivates me, and also helps me name things I would like to learn.

Asking this question has helped me be intentional about what sort of tasks, paid or volunteer, to which I can bring my best self. The trick for me has been in the practice, as in repeating it and making it habitual, because as I've made it a habit, it's become a default setting.

My own Examen also helps me better distinguish my growing edges and what are someone else's issues. This brings me a greater sense of hope because I can see what is in my capacity to influence, and what isn't. It also shows me what my non-negotiable values are in areas of justice, and inclusivity.

Framing the question is just the beginning. But where one starts impacts where one ends up.

DAY 16

God's Gifts

> Now we have received not the spirit of the world, but the Spirit that is from God, so that we may understand the gifts bestowed on us by God.
>
> 1 Corinthians 2:12

> Every generous act of giving, with every perfect gift, is from above, coming down from the Father of lights, with whom there is no variation or shadow due to change. In fulfillment of his own purpose he gave us birth by the word of truth, so that we would become a kind of first fruits of his creatures.
>
> James 1:17-18

At our house, Christmas was getting a bit out of control.

As parents, we relish giving our children gifts they enjoy. We try to balance our gift giving each year, between things that are fun and practical, indulgent and character-building. But we were getting carried away. Add in grandparents and neighbours, aunts and uncles, friends and cousins, and our tree was beginning to look like an explosion of stuff—much of which we didn't actually need.

One of our responses to that runaway consumerism, which so many other families experience at Christmas too, was to institute a new practice where we each make at least one gift for someone in our family. We draw names at the beginning of Advent, and create something really special for whoever we draw. We've exchanged hand painted t-shirts, homemade candles, cigar box ukuleles, and the ever popular coupon book for such meaningful gestures as chores, date nights, and hugs. Not only has this practice caused us to be more intentional and thoughtful with our gift-giving, it has led to some of the most memorable and cherished gifts under the Christmas tree each year.

The best gifts, I find, are a reflection of the giver. You can sense the investment in it. You can feel the time they pour into it. In the very best kinds of gifts, you can see the fingerprints of the giver. They're an expression of your relationship and an invitation into a shared future.

The Holy Spirit gives us these kinds of gifts. Sometimes they're called charisms, or spiritual gifts. There are lists of different kinds of spiritual gifts throughout scripture, for instance in Romans 12, 1 Corinthians 12, and Ephesians 4—gifts for things like encouragement, prophecy, healing, and evangelism, for instance. The scriptural lists are not exhaustive; any skill you possess might be a clue to your gifting, so long as it is a gift you can direct beyond yourself, towards the common good.

Spiritual gifts are the tools we use to contribute to God's project of bringing healing and wholeness to the world. In our various charisms and giftings, we see a glimpse of the Holy Spirit, the things Christ cares about, and the kind of future God is creating for the world.

If you have a gift for encouragement, it's because the Holy Spirit longs to see people encouraged and affirmed in God's love for them. If you have a gift for prophecy, it's because God has important truths that need to be spoken. If you have a gift for healing, it's because there is brokenness in the world that God longs to mend. If you have a gift for evangelism, it's because the Holy Spirit desires to draw people to God through you. If you have a gift for art, or communication, or empathy, or calculations... the list goes on and on and on... it's because the Holy Spirit wants you to use them for the building of God's kingdom.

In C.S. Lewis' novel *The Lion, the Witch and the Wardrobe*, Father Christmas bestows special gifts upon the four main characters (Lewis, p. 100). This is one of signs that the curse upon Narnia—a wicked spell that made it always winter, but never Christmas—is beginning to break. Father Christmas gives gifts of leadership, healing, protection, and assistance, in the forms of various swords, cordials, shields, and horns. These gifts become the tools, not only by which the Pevensie children are known, by through which they engage their various adventures and help liberate the land of Narnia from the rule of the White Witch.

The gifts that the Holy Spirit gives us are not solely for our benefit or enjoyment. They are meant to be used. They are glimpses of the common good and the new reality God is ushering in.

So cherish the gifts God has given you. Nurture them. Develop them. Give thanks for them. But above all, put them to use in ways that contribute to God's mission in the world. Your gifts are a sign of your belovedness. But even more so, they signify Christ's love of the entire world, and God's hopes for its future.

www.discoverment.org

Questions for Reflection:

When have you received a really meaningful gift? Who gave it to you? What made it so special?

When have you given a special gift to someone else? Describe what it feels like to give a gift that is well received. How do you think God feels about giving you your spiritual gifts?

My Daily Discoverment

Look up the lists of spiritual gifts cited in the Romans 12, 1 Corinthians 12, and Ephesians 4. Do any of the Biblical examples of spiritual gifts resonate for you? What do you suspect might be some of your spiritual gifts?

What might it look like to be a good steward of your spiritual gifts?

www.discoverment.org

DAY 17

Gifts and Proficiency

> Now there are varieties of gifts, but the same Spirit; and there are varieties of services, but the same Lord; and there are varieties of activities, but it is the same God who activates all of them in everyone. To each is given the manifestation of the Spirit for the common good.
>
> 1 Corinthians 12:4-7

When I was in primary school, my classmate Paul had the neatest printing in our class. The lines he made were perfectly straight, unlike the jagged scratches the rest of us made on the paper. His humps and bumps and swoops and loops were perfectly proportioned, graceful arcs; ours looked more like homemade pizza crust. The letters he formed were perfectly spaced and they all fit neatly in the pink and blue guide lines of his primary exercise book. The rest of us might as well have been in a university course on abstract art. We all knew Paul had a gift for printing. The teacher told us every day.

When I was in middle school, I remember a few of my friends were selected and taken out of our class for an afternoon each week, to participate in some specialized learning for gifted students. The rest of us never really knew what went on in that gifted program, but these friends sure made it sound like a very big deal, and enjoyed reminding us just how intellectually superior they were while we contested that the testing was flawed.

When I was in high school, I remember being asked at a friend's youth group to share something we were good at, by way of introduction. I remember not being able to come up with an answer that felt honest or true or affirming. I remember too, when I became a youth group leader myself, asking a handful of high school youth the same question, and being met with blank stares and awkward silence. Maybe I was no good at youth ministry either, I thought.

The reality is, we often have a really hard time seeing or claiming the gifts we possess or the things that we're good at. This, in spite of the fact that scripture tells us we are all gifted and equipped by the Holy Spirit for the building up of God's kingdom.

My sense is that there are three major obstacles to recognizing and claiming our giftedness: comparison, false humility, and perfectionism.

Comparison inaccurately inflates the giftedness of others and diminishes our own sense of value and belovedness. How many of us have felt worse about what we have to offer after fixating on the social media feeds of others? Comparison is always a losing game.

False Humility lets the insecurity of others diminish our own willingness to name and offer our gifts. Nobody likes a braggart. We often don't want to live into our giftedness because of the consequences we fear it might have for our relationships. False humility maintains the status quo.

Perfectionism lies to us by telling us that in order to be gifted at something, you have to be the very best at it. In our celebrity driven culture—that loves to lift up the stories of extraordinarily gifted people who make it big—there are millions who don't lean into what they're good at, because on TV there is someone who does it better. Perfectionism sacrifices the good gift, in search of the great.

Since things like comparison, false humility and perfectionism make questions of giftedness so difficult to answer, I want to lift up another word for us, that might get at it another way. That word is proficient. Instead of asking what you are good at, or what you are gifted in, try asking what tasks you are proficient at.

Proficiency is a level of expertise or ability that is elevated and exhibits competence, but it allows for lots of other people to be at that level with you. Proficiency is measured by one's ability to perform the task at hand, to do something well enough to be useful, not by one's ability compared to someone else's. Proficiency means being good at something, but also being good enough to not have to be the best. Proficiency is sometimes a God-given gift from birth, but more often it is attained by hard work, developing your gift, and honing your craft—in which case, the God-given gift is often one's determination to put in the time, effort and curiosity to achieve proficiency. And proficiency allows for a diverse community of people, who all are proficient in different ways, to recognize proficiency in others and nurture the potential in others without a spirit of competition or scarcity.

As you begin to articulate your deep gladness in life and the gifts entrusted to you by the Holy Spirit, ask yourself in what areas do you show proficiency for the work God has placed before you. And put those gifts to work. God gave them to you for a reason.

Questions for Reflection:

Who are the people around you—from your past or your present—who are lifted up for their giftedness? How do you respond when the people around you are lifted up? Have you ever been the one lifted up? Have you ever done the lifting? What goes through the mind of someone who is lifted up for their giftedness? What is going on in the heart of the people who lift up others?

When has comparison, false humility or perfectionism held you back from claiming your giftedness in Christ Jesus? When have these tendencies kept you from being able to celebrate the people around you?

What does the word proficient mean to you? How is it different from the language of giftedness? What does the notion of being "good enough" free up in you? In what areas do you feel either proficient or gifted for the work God calls you to?

Vocation has been described as the place where our deep gladness intersects with the world's needs. How does your sense of giftedness or proficiency nourish gladness deep within you?

DAY 18

Fully Alive

> "Prophesy to these bones, and say to them: O dry bones, hear the word of the Lord. Thus says the Lord God to these bones: I will cause breath to enter you, and you shall live. I will lay sinews on you, and will cause flesh to come upon you, and cover you with skin, and put breath in you, and you shall live; and you shall know that I am the Lord."
>
> Ezekiel 37:4b-6

Recently my wife found a good deal and bought me a second hand cordless drill. I'm not a super handy person—I still rely on the dollar store tool kit my parents bought me when I went off to university—so this felt like a definite step up in terms of power and possibility. The only problem was the rechargeable battery that came with it was dead and wouldn't charge. I cleaned off all the connector bits. I bought a new charging station for it. I wiggled it and jiggled it, and tried it in all the different plugs of our house. The thing just wouldn't charge. My new tool was useless and I was looking at having to buy a brand new battery which would've negated the good deal we got. That is, until I looked up a life hack on the Internet and found an ingenious way to jumpstart a rechargeable battery using simple household items. A couple copper wires, a 9-volt battery, a few moments of uncertainty later, and I was in business. I was pretty excited and proud of myself when my new-to-me drill sparked to life.

Are there things in life that make you come alive? What sparks creativity and imagination, passion, and curiosity within you? Think about those times when you get carried away in a conversation and time seems to fly by; when you get angry about something in a righteous way instead of just being annoyed; when you open your heart to something and are willing to risk disappointment. What is it that prompts those responses in you? And what clues might there be, revealing God's vocational invitation in our lives, as we experience ourselves fully alive in our world?

Howard Thurman, the Christian pastor and mentor to important civil rights leaders of the last century, drew the connection between our passions and vocations. He famously encouraged his hearers to become less fixated on what the world needs and instead seek out what made them come alive. For what the world truly needs, Thurman taught, is people who are fully alive.

Whatever it is that makes you come alive—that enlivens your spirit, that puts a spring in your step—is a sign pointing to the work God is calling you to engage. Particularly if you struggle to identify your gifts and proficiencies, start by claiming what makes you come alive first, then see how that intersects with the world's needs. The world needs people who are alive with possibility, not overburdened and overwhelmed by the needs that exist.

Some people come alive when they are able to use their gifts to their full capacity. Others come alive in pursuit of a meaningful cause or movement for justice. Some people come alive when they are given the freedom to be creative and innovative. Others come alive when there is structure and support around them to guide them in their efforts. Some people come alive in solitary endeavours, others in certain company. Some come alive in a role of nurturing those around them, while others come alive in situations of individual risk and adventure.

Whatever it is that makes you come alive, it is the alive version of you—not the beaten down, cynical, or begrudging version—that the world really needs. And when we pursue the things we are passionate about—when we bring more resiliency, creativity, perseverance, and effort into our work—we are more efficient and fruitful than when we slog our way through life-draining tasks.

Finding the thing that makes you come alive is a gift. It doesn't come by trying hard or having the right set of skills and abilities. It's not prescriptive or formulaic, and it won't be found in any list of life hacks on the Internet. It's a little like falling in love—you'll know it as you allow it to happen, as you lean in, and experience it.

Coming alive—in the work that we do and the things we pour ourselves into—is a gift from God, the Source of Life and is one of the ways we experience resurrection in our day to day lives.

Questions for Reflection:

Read Ezekiel 37. When have you experienced a "dry bone" season, when apathy and cynicism robbed you of life and vitality? Have you seen that in others? What has been helpful or unhelpful in such a season?

What makes you come alive? How is "coming alive" different from finding things that are simply fun and enjoyable? What do you find life draining? How is "life draining" different from things that are simply hard or challenging?

Reflect on the paraphrased teaching of Howard Thurman above. Why does he suggest the world so badly needs people who are fully alive?

What images or language or questions rise up for you when you imagine God as being the Source of Life? When Christians talk about the new life that is available in Christ, what do you envision? Where do you experience resurrection or new life in your world?

DAY 19

Passion and Enthusiasm

Greater love has no one than this: to lay down one's life for one's friends.

John 15:13 (NIV)

I appeal to you therefore, brothers and sisters, by the mercies of God, to present your bodies as a living sacrifice, holy and acceptable to God, which is your spiritual worship. Do not be conformed to this world, but be transformed by the renewing of your minds, so that you may discern what is the will of God—what is good and acceptable and perfect.

Romans 12:1-2

I know people who are deeply committed to veganism. They buy almond butter and oat beverage and talk your ear off about things like sustainability and animal cruelty and the like. I appreciate the vegan lifestyle and from time to time try to incorporate some of its practices, but to be honest, veganism has never captured my heart in a way that rouses much enthusiasm in me.

I know people who are really into politics. They read political biographies, they campaign for particular candidates and recruit memberships for a particular political parties. I try to stay current on the news and can articulate my broad political leanings, but to be honest, politics has never been something that's roused a whole lot of excitement in me.

I know people who are into music, physical fitness, design, conservation, fashion, child care, home renovations, and more. These are all worthy and potential-laden areas of life, in which God can be found and through which God can partner with us in amazing ways. One might argue that our common calling as Christians compels us to have at least a cursory investment in many of them.

It's so very wonderful when people find the one thing that stands above all others and makes them come alive. But I also know a lot of people who don't know what their "thing" is yet, or if they'll ever have a "thing" that sparks life within them. It can be a very uncomfortable place to be, waiting for something to grab hold of your heart, while other people around you are finding their niche in life. What about these people? Is God only calling out to you if you've found your "thing"?

Part of the challenge, I believe, is that we conflate the terms passion and enthusiasm.

Enthusiasm is when people are excited about something and seem to overflow with creative energy, joy, and curiosity about it. There is almost a giddy and childlike energy to people's enthusiasm.

Passion, however, is more a question of what you find valuable. It comes from the term "to suffer". In theological language, we talk about the Passion of Christ, or the suffering of Christ, when we tell the story of Jesus' death on the cross. When we speak of com-passion, we talk about entering into the suffering of another person, of empathy, of dying with someone else.

In her book *Practicing Passion: Youth and the Quest for a Passionate Church*, Kenda Creasy Dean describes how the mainline church has failed at showing young people a picture of a God that mattered and instead offered a lukewarm recipe for wholesome submissiveness. "Without something to die for," Dean explains, "adolescents have nothing to live for, either" (Dean, p. 33).

Passion is a value statement that says something is worth dying for, something is worthy of my life's commitment, something is worth building my life upon and giving my life for. Enthusiasm may or may not be part of the equation.

Jesus wasn't particularly enthusiastic about journeying towards the cross. In the Garden of Gethsemane he prayed for it to be avoided if at all possible. Yet, in the end, he relented and prayed for God's will to be done, because our relationship with God, our proximity to the Divine, was something he deemed worth dying for.

When the young men and women of a century ago volunteered to serve in the First and Second World Wars, and endured great hardships both at home and abroad, it was not in most cases with great enthusiasm, but with a firm belief that something was at risk that was worth dying for. When a young professional or student puts their ambitions on hold in order to care for a sick or needy family member, it is not done with enthusiasm, but out of a loving commitment to their loved ones. When a worldwide pandemic hits and people are forced to stay home, mask up, and modify their behaviour, it is not engaged enthusiastically, but with a steady conviction that our sacrifice is worth it to protect our community's most vulnerable. When we finally alter our dependency on fossil fuels and adopt more sustainable ways of walking this earth, it will not likely be with great enthusiasm but at great cost and with a deep resolve to care for the earth that is our home.

Passion identifies what is worth sacrificing our comfort, our safety, and sometimes our very lives for—so that our sacrificial living can be incorporated into the unfolding work of God to redeem and heal the world. Sometimes passion is accompanied by enthusiasm, and we find the thing that we enjoy and are good at and makes us come alive. Sometimes passion is marked with some reluctance—perhaps a sense of obedience and duty—and we need to summon the courage to do what is difficult, but right.

Either way, passion is about ascribing worth to something else, in light of the fact that God ascribes worth to us. We can live sacrificially and regard things as worth dying for, because Christ lived sacrificially for us and says we are worth dying for as well.

www.discoverment.org

Questions for Reflection:

How do you understand the difference between enthusiasm and passion?

Kenosis is a theological term for the outpouring of yourself. It's what we see exemplified in Jesus, especially in his incarnation (his coming to earth as a human) and his dying on the cross. What is something that you aren't enthusiastic about, but is worth pouring your life out for in sacrificial living?

How do you see words like obedience and duty and sacrifice fitting into your sense of calling and vocation?

What is the connection between being able to ascribe value to other people and causes, and the value you ascribe to yourself? How might being rooted in your belovedness help you to live sacrificially for others?

www.discoverment.org

****

BLOOM WHERE PLANTED
by Alydia Smith

I have always considered myself a resilient person, thanks to the strong and courageous people who have acted as role models and guides in my life, particularly my parents and family. From a young age I was taught to love and believe in myself, even if others (including society) did not. I was taught not to rely on the praise of others, for they might not have my best interests at heart. And I was taught that how God made me is not perfect, but just right. The stories my parents tell of me as a child are all stories of resilience and perseverance. I am told that when I was three, I was losing a tricycle race because my pedals were not working, so I picked up my tricycle, ran ahead of everyone, and sat back down in front of the child in first place and peddled to the finish line. Being resilient is part of my identity. I started my discernment process and went into ministry with this same perseverance, passion and resilience.

Within five years of starting the discernment process, I was shocked at how deflated and discouraged I felt about church ministry and my experiences (particularly experiences of discrimination and racism within the church). I may not have been "burnt out" but I certainly felt "used-up" and considered leaving the church several times. My commitment to my call (and perhaps my stubbornness) caused me to stay in the church (even though I was not always in what the church would classify as active ministry). I did stay, but I did not feel like I was when I started, a resilient, optimistic woman ready to bounce back from anything. I was hurt and deeply affected by my experience of ministry, as one of my friends described, "I lost some of my sunshine." I believed that God called me into ministry to offer my best, and although I was doing my best in the moment, I knew that it was not the best that I could offer.

At my lowest, I took on "bloom where you are planted" as a personal mantra. For me this statement meant to worship (praise and glorify God) in whatever circumstance I found myself. A plant offers worship through their beauty, fragrance, and work (that is, its contribution to the entire eco-system). The work of the blooming plant is worship. If I am allowing myself to bloom: being my best self, using my gifts and skills to God's glory, helping and contributing to the wider eco-system that I am a part of, then I, like the plant, am offering worship through my work where ever I am.

This understanding of worship and work as one has helped me to broaden my definition of ministry and has strengthened my commitment to my calling. I now picture myself as resilient seed, that is determined to bloom, regardless of where I am planted. This imagery has helped me to reframe some of the excrement that I have dealt with while discerning my call to ordained ministry. I have watched the crap become fertilizer over the years, and I know that my ministry does not need to look a certain way (it may actually look secular) to be valid. If I am offering worship in the spaces that I find myself, blooming where I am planted, I know that I am being faithful to my call.

www.discoverment.org

✳✳✳✳✳✳✳✳✳✳✳✳✳✳✳✳✳✳✳✳✳✳✳✳✳✳✳✳✳✳✳

DAY 20

Capacity and Limitations

Again, it will be like a man going on a journey, who called his servants and entrusted his wealth to them. To one he gave five bags of gold, to another two bags, and to another one bag, each according to his ability.

Matthew 25:14-15 (NIV)

When I was a little boy, I wanted desperately to be a part of our church's softball team. If you've ever participated in a church softball league, you'll know what an interesting mix it is of elderly parishioners on the physical decline, beer league ringers who've never been to church in their life, high school youth group members trying to impress their love interests, and over-zealous pastors whose pride in their church somehow hangs on the results of "non-competitive" softball scores. My high-school aged brother was on our church softball team, which meant I (as the younger sibling) got dragged to many of these games. Since I was too little to play, it was my job to cheer them on—a task, I felt was unworthy of my capabilities. Cheering meant being on the non-action side of the chain link fence. It meant listening to my mother talk to her church acquaintances. It meant I was sidelined, quite literally. So it wasn't long before I lobbied for, and eventually became, the team's batboy. And it wasn't long after that—after causing a few near collisions at home plate, and weeks of general nuisance making and being underfoot—that I was demoted again to cheer squad.

It is a real joy when we feel like we have something to give to an important cause. And it can be a real frustration when we bump up against, or have society define for us, our limitations. Both our capacity and our limitations have important things to teach us about our vocational callings.

Scripture is full of stories of people who contributed willingly towards God's work, out of their capacity and ability, whether big or small.

An elderly widow had a penny to offer. She may have wished she had more to give, but she was called to offer what she did have to the temple offering, and Jesus held her up as an example of great stewardship. A little boy had a lunch to share—some loaves and two fish. I imagine he felt his small offering wouldn't make a difference, but he was called to share what he did have with Jesus, and because of it we have a new and fuller sense of God's abundance. Moses, on the other hand, grew up in the Pharaoh's court. He had access to people in power and was able to gain an audience with the Pharaoh himself. Moses was called to use his capacity and privilege to set free his people, and because of it we know the real freedom that lies at the heart of faith. Solomon, from his riches, built the temple and gave the Israelites an anchor for their faith.

All of these people gave from their capacity, they had something to offer, and they gave it. Part of discerning our vocational call is to take stock of what it is we have to offer, and making it available for the unfolding of God's kingdom—whether it's a little or a lot.

But there is a gift in our limitations as well.

Sometimes our limitations are the closed doors, that point us to the actual door God is opening for us somewhere else. We know these limitations when we admit there are some things we simply cannot do—whether physically, emotionally, mentally or otherwise. There is a gift in being able to approach a limitation, and recognize there is important work for the building of God's kingdom, that is not mine to do. I had to admit, at some point in my life, that I would never be the starting goaltender for the Toronto Maple Leafs. I simply did not have, and did not hone, the ability to do so—though there are some years when they couldn't have done much worse. I also, in all likelihood, do not possess the capacity to be the leader of a nation-state, a jogger, a kindergarten teacher, a stock broker, a rodeo clown… the list (it's a long one) goes on and on and on. There is important work in this world that is not mine to do.

We can also know our limitations when we endure something we can do but that does not ignite joy in our souls. At some point in my high school years, I determined I could do science related subjects with some competency, but not with the same passion or energy that was sparked within me by the humanities. I could pursue a future in the sciences, math, or business—Lord knows the education system encouraged it—but I would likely end up being miserable to myself and those around me. This kind of limitation is perhaps trickier to discern, because I can transgress it for limited period—just like I can swim underwater while holding my breath—but not over the long haul. This kind of limitation, where we have the capacity but not the heart, requires us to know ourselves really well. We need to think deeply about what makes us tick, how our imagination works, and how God has gifted our heart and soul, not just our hands and feet.

Our society likes to feed us the line that we can be anything we want. This isn't only untrue when we think about our capacities to serve, it's also apparent that we shouldn't be anything we want. It's more important to discern what God wants from us than it is to pretend we live in a world without limitations. There is a gift in knowing our limitations as well as our capacity.

One last consideration. We live in a world that likes to define our limitations for us. Whether based on our gender identity, economic status, our physical or mental disabilities, or any other number of identity markers. Oftentimes the limitations the world identifies for us aren't limitations at all, but rather are conveniences that serve to perpetuate an unjust status quo. When people don't bother to make spaces accessible for people with mobility issues, when we neglect to address generational income disparity caused by injustices of the past, when circles of familiarity and privilege contrive glass ceilings that prevent the advancement of marginalized people, we create barriers between capable, called people and participation in the work they are called to engage. We are not using all the gifts God has entrusted to the world because we confuse our natural limitations with artificial barriers that need dismantling. The world suffers because of it.

Each one of us is a unique combination of our capacities and our limitations. Both are guiding us toward the work we are called to do. Part of that work is creating a world where all people can bring their full selves to the new thing God is doing in the world.

Questions for Reflection:

Name some of the gifts, resources, affinities, and access that you have to offer to God's work. Put some language to your capacity to serve. How does it feel when you know you are equipped and capable—the right person for the job—to address a particular challenge or opportunity?

Read the Parable of the Talents (Matthew 25:14-30). In it, each of the servants has a different capacity to serve, but they are each entrusted with the same task—to manage their master's wealth. Is it easier to serve faithfully when you have more capacity to do so, or is it harder? Why do you think the servant with the least capacity responds in the way he does?

Name some of your limitations. When did you discover them? What has been your experience of bumping into your limitations? What do your limitations speak to you about yourself? What might you need to adjust in order to be able to receive your limitations as a gift?

When have you bumped up against a barrier that prevented you from using your full capacity to serve? When have you erected a barrier, even unintentionally, because you couldn't be bothered to think creatively about accessibility? How might you need to think differently to be able to recognize and make use of the capacity we all hold?

My Daily Discoverment

✳✳✳✳✳✳✳✳✳✳✳✳✳✳✳✳✳✳✳✳✳✳✳✳✳✳✳✳✳✳✳

DAY 21

Signs of the Times

> Who knows? Perhaps you have come to royal dignity
> for just such a time as this.
>
> Esther 4:14b

When I was a child, my parents used to enjoy taking my brother and I to any pioneer village, historic house, national historic park or interpretive centre they could. All across North America, it seemed. If there was an opportunity to join a tour group, and ask long-winded, really precise questions of 20-something guides in period costume, my parents would go out of their way to subject us to that kind of experience. We assumed it was to build character in us, or develop an appreciation for the ways of our ancestors or something. But from my young perspective, once you'd seen one cabin, canon or horse-drawn carriage, you'd seen them all. I was more interested in the jar full of root beer flavoured candy sticks in the gift shop.

Now that I am an adult and have children of my own to subject to such things, I see things differently. Perhaps it's because I have a better understanding of the timeline of history and can place the different pieces of our shared story together. Perhaps it's because, having a greater number of years behind me and the ability to look back on the changes over my lifetime, I am now more appreciative of the passing of time. Perhaps it's because parents have a cruel way of inflicting on their children the kinds of hardships they had to endure themselves. None of those notions, however, explains how my imagination is stirred when I picture myself living in the past.

When I imagine myself living in a different time, I find my imagination isn't so much stirred by the prospect of using old technology like butter churns or wearing old clothes like petticoats and knickers, eating old food items or taking in old entertainment. I imagine, and it only takes a short demonstration of hand-washing laundry to know, all those things stunk. I wonder if what compels us isn't the question of how we might have responded to the needs and the issues of days gone by.

Would we have gone off to fight in the Great War? Would we have marched for peace and protested against Vietnam? Would we have stood up for civil rights in the 1960s, and women's rights in the 1970s, and honoured the treaties between Indigenous peoples and settlers during the years when places like Canada were being established?

Of course, in many cases the same issues that shaped the past continue to shape our present day as well, though they wear different costumes. The questions about having the courage to act, to stand up for justice and do what is right, are questions we can ask of ourselves today.

Can you recognize injustice? Jesus said that the poor will always be with you (Mark 14:7). The proverbs about the greedy and the power hungry are just as true today as they were in Biblical times. The discrimination, the delineation between Us vs. Them, the systems of racial and patriarchal and colonial injustice are just as evident today as they were in generations past, no matter how far we claim to have come. Lord, give us eyes to see.

And when we look at the needs of our time, may we see the movements of justice swirling around as well. The prophet Amos describes justice as rolling like a river and righteousness as a mighty stream (Amos 5:24). Jesus taught that he wind blows wherever it pleases, and so it is with people born of God's Spirit of justice (John 3:8). C.S. Lewis in his Narnia novels describes the Christ figure, Aslan, as being on the move (Lewis, p. 65). Justice is propelled forward by mighty movements in our society—it is not stagnant, sluggish or stationary. Do you have the courage to battle your own inertia and jump into the swirling currents?

How will God call to you in the midst of today's challenges and injustices? Amid things like unfettered capitalism, the environmental crisis, the need to challenge white supremacy, decolonize society, reconcile Indigenous and settler communities, and affirm that Black Lives Matter... God is still calling. Don't wait until they've made a national monument to the crises and movements of today. There is plenty of need, and imaginative responses at hand, if only we grab hold of the moment. If only we heed God's call.

My Daily Discoverment

Questions for Reflection:

What do you see as being the most crucial challenges of our time? Which of them do you feel particularly called to or equipped for? Do you feel enthusiastic about them or are you driven by something else?

Sometimes we develop a long term strategy to engage a cause over a lifetime—maybe this involves going to school or other forms of preparation for the struggle. But other times, the need is so urgent we can't put off our action any longer. What is your long term strategy and your short term strategy, for engaging the causes you feel called to?

Those who don't know their history are doomed to repeat it. What lessons from the past might we apply to today's challenges? What factors today have totally changed the landscape?

Sometimes we assume that the world is on an ever progressing march towards justice. But in recent years, we have experienced real regression in certain areas of public policy and discourse. What does it take to keep society moving towards justice? How can we ensure that we don't take steps backwards? What role might you have to play in the world's progression towards the Kingdom of God?

DAY 22

Vocation and Belonging

*For just as each of us has one body with many members,
and these members do not all have the same function,
so in Christ we, though many, form one body,
and each member belongs to all the others.*

Romans 12:4-5 (NIV)

But now thus says the Lord, he who created you, O Jacob, he who formed you, O Israel: Do not fear, for I have redeemed you; I have called you by name, you are mine.

Isaiah 43:1

Mary Kondo is a life consultant from Japan who sparked a certain form of minimalist craze a few years ago. I, along with many others, got caught up in her advice. Originating in the cramped urban spaces of Japan, Kondo's vision of living was one where people had fewer possessions and more spaciousness to enjoy the few things we hold onto. After only a few episodes of her show, I was rummaging through closets, culling my book collection, reorganizing my cupboards, and carting off to Goodwill or the recycling bin anything that didn't spark joy within me.

Mary Kondo—and other minimalist movements from living in tiny houses, to car shares, to up-cycling your décor—reminds us that life feels better when we really value the things that belong to us. It is a rejection of the consumerist culture we live in, that derives little fixes of happiness from accumulating more and more new stuff. There is a real difference between things that spark joy and things that provide a quick fix of disposable novelty.

As I seek to create a life that sparks joy in myself and others and God, I wonder then, to whom does my life belong? Does my life spark joy in anyone? Am I cherished? Am I worth holding onto, or am I leading a disposable quick-fix kind of life? Is the world already done with me?

Individualism tells me that my life belongs to me alone. I get to call the shots. I only need to look out for myself. The fact that we are so lonely and isolated from one another, in a world with so many people in it and so many tools for connection, is a testament to the shared belief that our lives belong only to us. Individualism runs rampant in our western society.

Scripture, however, reminds us that our lives do not belong to us alone. We belong to each other as well. Our stories cannot be extricated from the stories of our family, our community, our generation, etc. There are certain obligations upon me, certain responsibilities I hold, to care for my neighbour, the stranger, and the land upon which I walk. In Genesis 4, when Cain commits the ultimate act of individualism and murders his brother Abel, his shrugging off of responsibility comes in the form of a question to God. "Am I my brother's keeper?" The correct answer is, YES! You ARE your brother's keeper—just as he is yours as well.

Mother Teresa of Calcutta taught that If we lack peace, it is because we have forgotten our interconnectedness (Bojaxhiu). The African mutual care philosophy of Ubuntu helped South Africa emerge from years of apartheid. There are narratives we can choose to live by that reject the individualism of Western culture. The decisions I make have consequences beyond my own inner peace—they effect the peace of my community, the world around me, and Creation itself.

Since my life belongs to the people around me, it is also fair to say that the task of discerning my vocation does not belong solely to me as well. The people around me are an important resource to leverage as I open myself to God's call in my life. In different corners of the Christian tradition, this has looked like mentorship relationships, or cups of coffee with pastors, elders, friends and family. It can look like developing a connection to a spiritual director or spiritual accompanier—people who have training in how to listen for the Holy Spirit in the conversations you have and the reflections you share. It can look like a clearness committee or discernment group, where a team of people listen deeply and ask thoughtful questions that help illuminate insights you could never arrive at on your own. God has equipped each of us differently, and by coming together as the Body of Christ, we can do most things better, including listening for God's call on your life.

My Daily Discoverment

Remember too, that your life doesn't just belong to you, or your family, or your community or generation. In the end, your life belongs to God. And you spark much joy in your Creator.

Questions for Reflection:

One of the assumed tasks of emerging adulthood is to develop one's independence. Making your own money, paying your own bills, finding your own home have all been markers of what it looks like to be an independent adult. What is the difference, in your understanding, between independence and individualism? How might you pursue (or challenge) the developmental tasks of adulthood, without drifting into unhealthy individualism?

How do you respond to the notion that others—maybe family, community, or even God—have a claim to some aspects of your life? Do you think of the bonds you have to others as an anchor holding your back, or a collective holding you up?

Belonging to one another means we do not have to be amazing, or even sufficient, at everything. We can ask for help when we need it. How do you feel about asking for help from others? How do you feel when others ask for your help? How might the world be different if we truly felt we could call upon, and rely upon, each other?

Discernment is a team sport. What are the advantages and blessings to calling together a team of people to help you discern your vocation? Who might you call upon to assist you in this work? Make a plan to invite them into your discerning.

www.discoverment.org

****

YOU ARE NOT ALONE
by Karen Orr

As I look back on my earlier years, I wish I had understood more of what discernment really meant and its importance. I wish I had someone to journey with me during decisions. Now as a spiritual director, I see how valuable it is to have someone with you on the journey and what a joy it is to journey with someone.

I wish everyone could find a spiritual director. Spiritual directors journey with people as they work through life and vocational choices. We are not the "directors"—God is! As a spiritual director, my job is to listen and illuminate where God is at work in your life. I watch for patterns, new perspectives, I offer prayer, I lead you in spiritual practices and I affirm where God is actively working in your life.

My own director has seen me through vocational discernment decisions. She sees how sometimes I get stuck and what helps me get unstuck. For example, at some point every year I get frustrated with my ministry job and think it's time to quit. She was the one who illuminated to me that this pattern happens every spring. So now when it happens, rather than thinking of resigning, I ride it out, knowing now that it will pass. God still wants me to continue, I am just weary. Without her, I would have changed jobs every spring. She reminds me to stay true to who God has created me to be. She challenges me to have quiet time with God, to hear God's quiet voice in my life.

If a trained spiritual director isn't for you, hopefully you are blessed with a mentor or a treasured friend in your life that will journey with you in discernment. I also have two close friends, who will tell me something I am missing in my decisions, or remind me that I really am gifted in that particular area when I feel like a failure. The point is we are not meant to walk this path alone.

In some churches, discernment committees are set up when one is contemplating a vocation in ministry. The purpose of the committee is to walk alongside the person to affirm gifts, talents, and to again see where God is working in their life. The committee doesn't tell them the answers but gently guides the person to help them hear from God. Wouldn't it be great if we all had a group of people in our lives helping us make important vocational decisions? It has always been my hope that congregations will rally around young people (or anyone really) and walk with them to help them discern vocations.

In my work as a youth minister, I see young people struggling to make vocational decisions. Things get muddled when you add in what your parents want you to do, what your grandparents think you should do, what others are doing, or what great money you could make (even if you don't like the career choice). So I see this as a perfect time to have a spiritual director, a mentor or a trusted friend, or a group of people to illuminate the journey for you.

My prayer is that as you read this, you will be inspired to seek out a spiritual director, a beloved friend, a mentor or a community you trust! Or perhaps you will be the friend or mentor to someone walking this journey!

www.discoverment.org

****

DAY 23

Vocational Seasons

> For everything there is a season, and a time
> for every matter under heaven.
>
> Ecclesiastes 3:1

Sometimes my wife and I dream about the different places where we could live. She dreams about living in some seaside cove on a Greek island. I dream about living in the misty moors of Scotland or Ireland. My wife has dual citizenship—Canada and the USA—so we have sometimes wondered if there were places down south where we might feel called to set up shop. Usually when we pontificate about such things, we end up back where we began, listing off the myriad reasons we have to be thankful for where we are currently. One of the reasons we fall back on is that we long to live somewhere where we can experience all four of the seasons.

Seasons are one of those things that mark the cycle of time and the deepening of one's life. Seasons are cyclical. Seasons are rhythmic. We can envision how to live in one season based on our experience of that same season in times past. I would love to be one of the old-timers one day, who can recall how high the snow got on the telephone pole some winter thirty years back, or how dry the fields were from some summer in my youth. If we lived somewhere that didn't experience the four seasons to their fullest, I don't feel my life would be rooted in quite the same way.

Of course there are different kinds of seasons that people use to mark their lives, beyond the natural seasons of winter, spring, summer, and fall. I know a number of student athletes on our campus who are so committed to the life of athletics, that they pace out their lives to the rhythm of sports seasons—off-season, pre-season, regular season, and playoffs. People who live closer to the land than I do may pace out their lives by hunting seasons, the migrations of different animals across the land, cycles of the moons, or the mating seasons of different animals. Even the seasons we binge-watch on Netflix have a predictable arc to them—from season premiere to season finale—that shape our expectations, and pull us forward in the story, until we realize it's 3am and we have an 8:30am class in the morning. In the church, we have the cycle of the liturgical seasons—from Advent and Christmas, through Lent and Easter, and then Pentecost and (the ever exciting) Ordinary Time—that tell and retell the stories of Jesus and the early church.

Just as the snow comes in winter and hockey players grow beards during playoffs, so too do our vocational callings take different forms over different seasons of our lives.

Sometimes our vocational season changes because we grow or diminish in our abilities, knowledge, or capacity to serve. Sometimes our vocational season changes because some new need in the world emerges and we are called to respond. Sometimes our vocational season changes because our passion or enthusiasm or perspective on something changes, or because we discover a new gifting in an area we didn't know we had. Sometimes a new opportunity opens up out of nowhere, and we can't quite articulate why we are drawn to it, apart from a sense that the Spirit is calling.

Your sense of vocation will likely change over the course of your life. That's okay. If we are truly listening for God's voice, we can embrace the changes and learn from the different seasons God leads us through. We may even find that the gifts and lessons and experiences from one season prepare us in ways we would never have imagined to serve faithfully and imaginatively in another—even if the work looks completely different. God's call over the course of our lifetimes can sometimes looks more like a zig zag than a linear progression, which can frustrate parents and guidance counsellors and academic advisors. What the world calls stopping and restarting, and laments as vocational indecisiveness, can actually look like deepening faithfulness when we seek to respond to God's call over the different seasons of life.

The real gift of old age is the ability to look back on your life's seasons, and see patterns and themes that emerge with perspective. Sometimes we are too close to see the patterns and wisdom that emerges in real time. Isn't it great then, to be able to draw upon the elders around us, who have lived through more seasons than we have. And to trust in the God who is the author of all the seasons in our lives. For even though the seasons change, we belong to a God whose love for us is constant and whose hopes for the world is unchanging.

Questions for Reflection:

How would you identify the different seasons of your life so far? Are they marked by certain contexts, or relationships, or roles, or something else? How has your sense of who you are and what you are called to do changed over the course of those seasons?

Some people will identify different seasons that mirror the natural seasons. We experience winter seasons, where life is still, at rest, and anticipating what comes next. We experience spring seasons, that are full of new life and possibility. We experience summer seasons where life is in full bloom, and autumn seasons where things are winding up and concluding. Which of these seasons feels truest to your experience right now? What might you need from God or from others, to live fully into that season? What might you keep in mind as you meditate on the seasons that are just around the corner?

Seasons change. Think back on some of the changes that have happened in your life. What helps you to navigate change? What keeps you grounded and secure in the midst of change? What might help you to embrace the changes that will inevitably come? As vocational seasons change, what remains the same?

How do you respond to people who will question or be critical of the vocational changes over your lifetime? Whose feedback do you value? Whose do you dismiss? As you sense a change in vocational seasons, who might you go to for help discerning?

My Daily Discoverment

****

A CLOSET FULL OF OPTIONS
by Kimberly Ivany

I've always loved writing.

When I was in grade two, I would flip my notebook eight pages ahead and make a star on that eighth page: "I am going to write my story to here!" I would say to my classmates.

And I would.

I loved the magic of words filling up the page; the fascinating process of watching my penciled ideas create a new world from my own imagination.

That love for the craft stuck with me until Grade 12 when it came time to pick what program I wanted to pursue in university.

I ended up going to Ryerson University for journalism. Thanks to an internship in my fourth year, I was able to start at the Canadian Broadcasting Corporation as a casual employee right after school in 2012.

But after nearly four years of jumping contract to contract, and pushing myself through so much stress in newsroom roles that did not feed my soul, I was feeling a pull to something else.

I asked myself this question many times when work felt unbearable: What are the parts I love about journalism—and what can I do with them? I love writing. I love people. I love listening to people's stories and sharing them. I love public speaking and I love fighting for social justice. I also really love the Divine. A United Church pastor—just like my Dad—seemed like the perfect fit for my heart.

I began seriously exploring this desire through concerted discernment classes.

A common reaction surfaced when I would tell people what's up: "But you don't need to become a PASTOR to partake in ministry!" many people would say. "You can be a minister wherever you are."

I would get so annoyed every time someone said it: "Yes but—I WANT to be a minister."

I'm not sure if I did ever reply to the naysayers that forcefully, but I certainly felt it. After all, this path to being a minister was my new trajectory, and no one could tell me otherwise... except God, of course.

It came to pass, through those classes and talking with God through the process, that 2015 was not the right time to pursue formal ministry.

Amazingly, at the same time, my journalism career was on a slow and steady incline. And about a year later, those surging opportunities blossomed into a full time job at CBC's *The Fifth Estate*, Canada's premier investigative documentary program.

Through my investigative work at the CBC, I've told stories about the unsolved cases of missing and murdered Indigenous women and girls in Canada. I have held the government to account when they let multi-millionaire tax cheats off the hook. I've been the voice for Ontario Provincial Police officers suffering from PTSD, demanding better care in their workplace. I've shone light on hidden science that proves seatbelts in school buses are actually safer for kids.

Those people from the earlier part of my journey were correct. As a journalist, I tangibly see the ways in which I am amplifying the Kingdom of Heaven on Earth.

That being said, I actually haven't closed the door to church ministry completely. And in truth, there are most certainly times in my job when I feel detached from the breadth of my skill set and passions. Those times are very real.

But that's the thing about vocation. It does not necessarily cement itself as one thing forevermore. There are no rules in how our vocation takes shape, nor how the Divine talks with us and leads us.

It is indeed affirming when we know we are wearing the best pair of shoes in the closet. But heck—I've got more outfits and 10 more pairs in there that I want to try on too.

My Daily Discoverment

✶ ✶

DAY 24

Multiple Callings

His master said to him, 'Well done, good and trustworthy
slave; you have been trustworthy in a few things,
I will put you in charge of many things;
enter into the joy of your master.'

Matthew 25:21

Here in Canada where I live, when it gets cold the wisest people dress in layers. There is no such thing as bad weather—I've heard from a previous parishioner—only people who make bad decisions about what to wear. This person was a high school gym teacher who loved encouraging people to get outside and be active. Dressing in layers is perfect for active living, because if you get too hot, you can shed a layer, or if you get too cold you can add another layer on top.

Since God is active in the world—and the world can be a cold, harsh place—I've found there have been seasons where God layers up multiple vocational calls in my life, multiple areas where I have felted compelled, equipped, and led to serve.

My sense of vocational calling, in my adult years at least, has always centred around the spiritual care of young people. This has taken different forms as I have engaged different opportunities with congregations, camps, denominational bodies, and now at a university campus. In my first youth ministry job, I used to stay late at our church producing elaborate newsletters (back before social media) decorating intricate bulletin boards (this may have been at the tail end of the flannel graph era), and cutting out doodles from the clipart book for the church bulletin (yes, this was before Google image search). I was single, had no children, and could pour a tonne of time and energy into the important work I knew God was calling me to.

Then I wasn't. I got married. We had kids. I entered a new season of my life. And for some reason, I wasn't staying at the church until 2am anymore. My vocational life was shifting. Or perhaps more accurately, God was adding new layers to the ways in which I was being called to love and serve. I feel just as passionately called to the work I do as a husband and a father as I do to the work God still calls me to do with the church. And for the most part, those two callings work well together—except when they don't, and I have to reevaluate the boundaries between them.

We live in a society where the needs of employment and home and community are all crying out to us. Our society likes to lift up examples of people who can do it all—career, family, volunteering, etc.—and look good doing it. Even in ministry circles, we hear more and more about ministers who are bi-vocational (they serve a church part-time and have another side gig that pays the bills) or co-vocational (they serve a church and have another calling which they are also passionate about). Some people see the added layers as a burden or impediment. Others love the way their various callings complement and inform each other.

It is okay if you feel God calling you to more than one area of work at a time. It can be challenging and might pull you in different directions, but God will give you what you need... including a sense of boundaries.

It is okay if you feel God calling you to pour yourself into one single thing—be it parenting, or employment, or caring for the vulnerable, or whatever. Sometimes it is a gift to have a singular focus in life.

Both are okay because the call originates with God, not us. If we feel pulled in different directions because we're trying to please everyone or live up to some impossible standard put before us by society, then we're not living into our vocation, because those calls do not come from God. But on the other hand, if we limit our vocational imagination to one thing and one thing only, we might be missing out on some of the richness of the life God has in store for us, and causing others to suffer needlessly.

In the book of Acts, we hear that Paul—along with being an apostle for the Gospel—was also a tentmaker. Sometimes I wonder how Paul felt about his tent-making. Was he passionate about it? Did he feel called to it? Did he pray over the fabric and the stitching and the tent poles? Did he see it as a way to serve the people God brought his way? Or was it simply a way to pay the bills, so he could pursue the work he actually felt called towards? Does it matter? Part of me wants to see Paul as someone who saw meaning and calling and spiritual opportunity in every aspect of his life. But part of me also thinks there is something wonderful and holy about earning a paycheque, showing up for work, and putting a boundary around your work life so you can pour your heart into what you do outside of employment. To me, both feel like possible ways to honour a call.

www.discoverment.org

Questions for Reflection:

Some people like to focus on one project at a time. Others are able to divide their attention and contribute to multiple areas of work simultaneously. Which sounds more like you? What are the gifts of that approach to work? What are some of the challenges or limitations of it?

This reflection uses the image of layering multiple articles of clothing, in order to respond to changing conditions. What is freeing or encouraging about the idea of adding or removing different vocational calls? What is unnerving about it?

What is the difference between experiencing multiple vocational callings, and feeling pressure to "do it all?" When might you know if you're experiencing one or the other? Is there a difference between multi-tasking and having multiple vocational callings?

Sometimes people put up a boundary around their vocational life in order to distinguish between the work they feel called to and the work that allows them to pursue that calling. What boundaries do you put up around the different areas of your life? Are those boundaries hard and rigid, or are they porous and flexible? How do we allow God into all aspects of our life, even if we think differently about certain aspects of it?

www.discoverment.org

****

DAY 25

General and Specific Callings

> There is one body and one Spirit, just as you were called to one hope when you were called; one Lord, one faith, one baptism; one God and Father of all, who is over all and through all and in all. But to each one of us grace has been given as Christ apportioned it.
>
> Ephesians 4:4-7 (NIV)

Sometimes I have conversations with university students about whether or not they should pursue more schooling after they graduate. Pursuing a master's degree or a doctorate are sometimes things people feel called to on their vocational journeys. Education can be an important season in which people prepare for the work that is theirs. Sometimes degrees and certificates unlock accreditations that allow us to do God's work in the world. University or college education can be an important investment in your vocation, and the research that academics do adds to our knowledge and moves forward important advancements in our world.

We sometimes, however, conflate people's value or worth or intellect with the number of degrees they have, as if the letters behind someone's name or the honorific in front were merit badges or medals. The truth is, staying in school longer doesn't necessarily make you wiser or more valuable or even more employable. In many cases, it simply makes you more of a specialist.

Specialists aren't any more special than you or me. They simply have a calling or an interest or feel drawn to a singularly narrow field of study. So if you are absolutely compelled to find out how many angels can fit on the head of a pin, or on the right way to fit a camel through the eye of a needle… then maybe further schooling is an important step to take. There can be value in diving deeply into a narrow course of study, if it is relevant to God's healing work in the world—which I doubt is the case in either of the topics listed above. But maybe you'll convince me.

On the other hand, there are people who have specialized themselves right out of employability, or polite conversation, or usefulness to anyone at all. Maybe you've seen people like this—who get so engrossed in a specific area of interest that they have difficulty relating to the rest of the world. Sometimes we talk about the virtue of a long obedience in the same direction; Eugene Peterson wrote a book by that title, all about the long haul of a life of following Jesus. But a long obedience is no virtue at all if you're pointed in a meaningless direction to begin with. Travelling far down the road of obscurity, or vanity, or personal pet projects is futile if your journeying isn't pointed in the direction of the common good.

Some people, such as David Epstein in his book *Range*, argue that generalists—people who study or engage in a wide variety of different areas without venturing too deeply—are better equipped to engage with the difficult problems of today's complex world. The development of new technologies, for instance, requires people conversant in the ethical dilemmas these new technologies open up. The global economy needs business people who can navigate different cultures and languages. Being a generalist often provides the range of proficiencies and perspectives needed to address the real objective of our learning—the service of the common good.

The reality is, before the pediatrist or the paediatrician or the gerontologist or the heart specialist found their calling, they were a doctor first. They took an oath—to do no harm, keep confidentiality, etc.—common to all in their field, and are bound by their commonalities first, before leaning into their specializations. Before they were math teachers or philosophy teachers or gym teachers or science teachers, the best educators you know were bound by a common vision of what it means to teach. Before they were pitchers or catchers or third basemen or middle relievers, the athletes you know of were captured by a love of the game and an identity as baseball players, or athletes, or simply human beings.

Before we discern or grow into our specialized callings, we first must respond to and bind ourselves to our general calling as Christians. Our shared Christian calling binds us to things like unconditional love of God and neighbour, self-giving love, and sacrifice as modelled for us in Jesus, respect for the environment and stewardship of Creation, among others.

Our specific callings—the vocational pathways we discern—do not give us a free pass on the obligations bound to us by our general callings as Christians. If you discern a specific call to upfront leadership (say in a faith community or other organization), it does not entitle you to get caught up in your ego: our general calling as Christians won't allow it. If you discern a call to care for your family or loved ones, it does not entitle you to neglect your neighbour or the strangers whom God loves in other parts of the world: our general Christian calling has an outward focus as well. If you discern a call into business, it does not entitle you to do business in a manner which exploits the poor or spoils the environment: our general Christian calling requires we do business differently.

In describing our shared Christian calling to live out God's preferential option for the poor, for example, John Neafsey writes, "the word 'option' is not meant to suggest that solidarity with and commitment to the poor is 'optional.' Actually, it is seen as essential and integral to the Christian life" (Neafsey, p. 148).

Much as we might like to, we cannot simply opt out of participation in many areas of the world's brokenness—economic disparity, environmental degradation, or racial injustice, for instance. We are participants whether we realize it or not. In situations like this, if we attempt to opt out, our silence only serves to maintain a status quo of oppression and harm.

"All of us are called to opt for the poor," writes Neafsey, "to open our hearts to the poor, to do something with our lives that will make a difference for the better in theirs. The secret to salvation, to realizing our full humanity, is to find our own way to exercise this option in a meaningful way" (Neafsey, p. 149).

We are Christians first—with all the demands and obligations that places on us. We are called to a specialized piece of God's redemptive work second. They are two sides of the same coin. Together they make up our calling, our invitation, to participate in God's work of healing and reconciliation.

Questions for Reflection:

What are some good reasons for going deep into academics? What are some less-than-good reasons? What does academic study prepare you for? How do you know when you've been in school long enough?

What is an example of a narrow field of study that is tied to the common good? How can you tell if your studies are tied to the common good, or if they're simply indulging your own interests and appetites?

Why might a generalist be better equipped to address certain complex problems facing the world today? What kinds of problems would you rather have a specialist address?

What do you think is involved in being a Christian? What obligations or affirmations does it bind you to? Can you think of someone who might have a conflict or tension between their specialized calling and their general calling as a Christian? How might they resolve that tension?

My Daily Discoverment

✳✳✳✳✳✳✳✳✳✳✳✳✳✳✳✳✳✳✳✳✳✳✳✳✳✳✳✳✳✳✳✳

THE CALL TO LEARNING
by Margaret Propp

To go to university, college, technical school, special training for the career you have in mind… it's a difficult decision when there are so many things to consider.

What do I want to do? Who do I want to be? What do I want to get out of my learning? What's even possible?

I didn't really have a choice about whether I wanted to go to university. As a child of first generation immigrants, and my parents working labour jobs, the expectation was that all my siblings, including me, would get a degree so we could become 'professionals.' All four of us took out student loans and managed to finish degrees, with two of us doing our masters. I did well in high school, but my strong subjects were math and science. I think having to learn English as a second language growing up made classes like English and social studies hard because my reading and writing skills had not been 'mastered' yet. This made subjects that didn't require much reading or writing like math and chemistry easier. My highest marks were in chemistry, so I thought that was what I should take in university. I soon figured out that even though I was good at chemistry, I did not enjoy it. Instead I took an art and art history class, and loved it! I was torn because after 2 years of chemistry courses, I had found something I loved. In the end, I'm not doing either major from my first degree. I ended up going to seminary and getting my Masters in Divinity and becoming a campus chaplain and parish pastor. And get this, I have to write a sermon (which is like an essay) every week!

Care For Creation

For many students, the path is not so clear. Often students are not sure what the end goal is—not sure if going to school is what they want or need. And certainly school is not for everyone. But learning is a vocation that we are all called to participate in. In the same way we are called to care for God's creation of our earth, our bodies, our neighbours… caring for our minds through life-long learning is caring for God's creation.

Being In Community

Depending on your living situation, going to school can involve more than just text book learning—it can also develop the basic life skills of living on your own. A significant part of one's learning comes from the community you are a part of, fellow classmates, roommates, clubs, student services, or connecting with a chaplain and a community of faith. The late nights quizzing each other. Having conversations after a lecture on what was discussed in class. Don't underestimate the informal time you have with different people as part of the learning process.

Forgiveness

To try things that may result in failure is part of the learning. In a world that puts value on success and progress, it may be difficult to accept failure. You may be ashamed of it. We are called as people of faith to live in forgiveness and this also means for ourselves. In our discovery of ourselves, there are many distractions and opportunities to be self-indulgent, without the restrictions set by parents or other influences we grew up with. Part of the learning is discerning the boundaries we want to set for ourselves around alcohol, drugs, sex, and media consumption. We can experience pleasure and freedom, but there is always the danger of excess that can result in addiction, unhealthy and risky behaviour. Talk to people you trust and respect so you can have some healthy conversations regarding some of these decisions.

Learning to Love

Finally, when you love what you are doing, it is usually a pretty strong indication that you are being faithful to your call. God promises to give us life and life abundantly. Pay attention to the places, people, and subjects that expand your sense of life. Loving life usually results in joy, and this is something that hopefully you can experience in your vocation as a student.

DAY 26

Our Relationship to Work

> The Lord God took the man and put him in
> the Garden of Eden to work it and take care of it.
>
> Genesis 2:15 (NIV)

> Whatever you do, work at it with all your heart,
> as working for the Lord, not for human masters.
>
> Colossians 3:23 (NIV)

Love what you do—the old saying goes—and you'll never work another day in your life.

This bit of advice is attributed to a wide range of people. Everyone from Marc Anthony, to Mark Twain, to business writers and motivational speakers. It was even spouted as a bit of down-to-earth country wisdom by the character Wayne on the comedy series *Letterkenny*. It almost sounds like it could be in the Bible. Except that it's not entirely true, I find.

Finding your vocation, the area of work God is calling you to participate in, the work that you love and feel passionate about and are gifted in and called towards, does not mean there won't be days that feel like a lot of struggle, effort, frustration and disappointment. God does not call us to a life of ease and enjoyment; we are called to a struggle, a healing work that involves effort and sacrifice and the sweat of our brow over a long period that won't always feel like progress. As one church leader put it to me when I was a young youth minister complaining about the hardships I faced in my ministry: that's why they call it work, and not super-fun-happy-time.

As we listen for God's calling, we sometimes confuse our vocation with a life of ease and fulfillment, easy results and enjoyable colleagues. Sometimes young people entering a new vocational season feel entitled to perks and privileges that they haven't yet earned, and see any bump in the road as a sign of being outside their vocational calling. But more often than not, the work God calls us into requires patience, resilience, perseverance, and effort.

As we listen for God's calling in our lives, we would do well to explore our assumptions about work. Many Christians assume that work is an unfortunate consequence or God-inflicted punishment on human beings, that exists only because of the Fall—after Adam and Eve disobeyed God. But if we look at the Eden story, we see that Adam (and presumably Eve) worked in the garden before they were deceived by the serpent. They laboured to harvest the fruits of the garden. They worked creatively to observe and name the different animals. Work was part of the human experience of God's perfect garden—and I imagine there were aspects of their work that the first humans struggled with, were frustrated by, and that didn't come easy. There may have even been days where Adam and Eve wanted to call in sick—had sickness been a thing yet.

Work is part of what makes us human. It's part of what we were designed for.

The key difference between work in the garden and work after the Fall, is the proximity of God to the work we are doing. In the Garden of Eden, God works right alongside Adam and Eve. They are in relationship with one another. They take coffee breaks together. They struggle together and are creative together and nothing is hid from each other. After the Fall, a whole lot of greed and abuse and power imbalance gets cemented into our working systems. The environment becomes something to exploit, rather than a gift to steward wisely. The fruit of our labour feeds a prosperous few, rather those who work hardest or need it the most. The brokenness of the world makes it harder to see God and God's purposes in our work.

When we feel isolated from our labour—which often happens when we become part of a labour system that treats us like cogs in a machine instead of bearers of the image of God—and when we feel isolated from our co-workers and ourselves and the Divine, we can easily begin to feel cynical about our work, like it has no meaning or value, and is something to avoid. Knowing the *why* of our work—rooting it in the mission of God—reconnects us with all the things our economic systems alienate us from—purpose, community, and the One who calls us. Do you want to spill yourself out in ways that maintain an unjust status quo? Or do you want to pour your efforts and energy into the new reality God is creating?

Not only do we need to feel connected to a meaningful purpose of our labour, our labour also needs to be balanced with rest and worship and play. Self-care is the important work—and it is work—that most corporations do not budget adequately for. Many of the world's systemic problems can be traced back to runaway capitalism, how it isolates us from a meaningful purpose for our labour, and forces us to live unbalanced lives.

As you discern a vocational identity and distinguish your calling from the trappings of capitalism, may you love the work you are called to do, at least enough of the time to keep at it. May you love the One who calls you to that work, even if every once in a while you question or doubt or shake a fist in God's direction. May you love the world you are called to do it for, in all its beauty and need and complexity. And may you have resiliency for when that work is difficult and discouraging.

www.discoverment.org

Questions for Reflection:

Think about the work you feel called to do. What is it you love about it? What aspects of it do you not love? What sustains you through the parts that feel discouraging? What roots you in the "why" of your work?

Read 2 Thessalonians 3:6-12 and its warnings against idleness. What are some of the pitfalls of avoiding work and living a life of ease? How do you distinguish between idleness and forms of work that are less obvious, such as intellectual work or internal work or restorative self-care?

The Protestant Work Ethic is a narrative that turned the acceptance of hard work into a type of spiritual virtue. What is so virtuous about hard work and struggle? What does it develop in us? Does it reflect God's character and hopes for us, or not? How can turning hard work into a spiritual virtue be taken advantage of by people in power?

Where have you noticed the challenges that capitalism poses for a meaningful understanding of work? What other systems misshape our sense of meaningful work in the world? How might you need to challenge or reinterpret those systems in order to claim your vocational identity?

www.discoverment.org

****

DAY 27

Vocation and Ministry

> The gifts he gave were that some would be apostles, some prophets, some evangelists, some pastors and teachers, to equip the saints for the work of ministry, for building up the body of Christ, until all of us come to the unity of the faith and of the knowledge of the Son of God, to maturity, to the measure of the full stature of Christ.
>
> Ephesians 4:11-13

The first job I ever had was when I was a young teenager, cutting grass for our church. We had a big old church building on the main street of our town—a classic Wesleyan Methodist brick barn with a steeple and rose window and a spacious front lawn. The lawn is where people posed for wedding pictures, where community groups held yard sales as fundraisers, and where each year our Sunday School leaders put on a vacation bible school with crafts, games, and a dunk tank on the final day. The church custodian, who was elderly enough to not want to cut grass in the heat, hired me to come by once a week (or more if it needed it) to cut the front lawn and a few other spots surrounding the church. It was my first experience of earning a pay cheque, being trusted with a set of keys, and having to keep track of submitting the hours that I worked.

I took a good bit of pride in my lawn cutting responsibilities. I knew that the front lawn of our church was one of the windows out into the wider community. If it looked shabby it would reflect poorly on us. I took care to have it looking good—and to be out of the way—for any weddings, funerals, or other big occasions at the church. I remember on one occasion, cutting the lawn so the pattern of the cross might be discernible in the grass, should any airplanes fly overhead and wonder what we were about. I don't know that I was particularly enthusiastic about lawn care, but I took care to do the best I could and wanted my work to be a reflection of my church community and the God we served. And though my picture never appeared on the staff directory of our church, it would not be too far a stretch to say I thought of my work each summer as part of our church's ministry, and maybe even a little ministry unto itself.

One of the great contributions of the German theologian and church reformer Martin Luther to the church's understanding and practice of vocation, is his notion that all vocations are a form of ministry. His emphasis on the priesthood of all believers revolutionized the way the church of his time thought about vocation. Back then, and even in some church traditions today, when you spoke of having a vocation, you were talking about a vocation to the priesthood, the monastery, or some other form of institutionalized leadership within the church. All other forms of occupation and work were deemed temporal, secular, and of less importance than the spiritual work of church leaders.

Luther, who was no big fan of church leadership in his time, opened our notions of vocation by claiming spiritual legitimacy for the work that happens outside of the institutional church. In his 1520 open letter to his German supporters, he wrote:

> *It is pure invention that pope, bishops, priests and monks are to be called the "spiritual estate"; princes, lords, artisans, and farmers the "temporal estate". That is indeed a fine bit of lying and hypocrisy. Yet no one should be frightened by it; and for this reason—namely, that all Christians are truly of the "spiritual estate," and there is among them no difference at all but that of office… Christ has not two different bodies, one "temporal," the other "spiritual." He is one Head, and He has One body.* (Luther as quoted in Placher, 211-213)

The work that happens beyond the institutional church is packed with just as much spiritual value, importance and potential, as the work that goes on within it.

That said, there are some people whom God calls to take on the important work of church leadership. Lillian Daniel and Martin B. Copenhaver have written a lovely book, titled *This Odd and Wondrous Calling* that gives a beautiful glimpse into what the work of ministry is like, both its challenges and its joys. Just the title itself gives a clue as to the nature of the calling—simultaneously odd and wondrous—and it's a privilege to receive that kind of calling. I'll share just a few thoughts from my own experience, for those who may be wondering if such a calling is being gifted to them.

1. Church leadership is about building up the Body of Christ so that the whole community can find opportunities to serve in the world; it's not about pursuing your own personal agendas or projects. Make sure you engage a call to ministry from a place of wanting to equip others for the ministry, the vocation, that God calls them to, not just to enact your own ideas or preferences about what you think the church can or should look like.

2. Church leadership is changing. Listen to the wisdom of ministers who have gone before, but know that skills such as creativity, risk-taking and entrepreneurship will be a bigger part of the post-Christendom work of ministry than was previously. Your ministry will be unique to you and to the context and times to which you are called. Trust the ways that God has equipped you for ministry in this day and age. Appreciate, but don't feel too beholden to, the patterns of the past.

3. Ministers are called first and foremost to the *work* of ministry, not to a position or an institution. At their best, church institutions can be an expression of community, helping you live into your calling and supporting you as you engage important work. At their worst, they can be full of gatekeepers and obstacles, battlegrounds for power games, and unwitting perpetuators of things like racism, sexism, homophobia, and more. Church institutions like to set up lots of checks and balances over who can be a "minister" and who can't. Approach the process with patience and humility. Know that the discernment and pursuit of your calling may require perseverance, patience, and some thick skin. You may need to work hard to find the right fit for your gifts and calling; it's not always in the denomination where you were raised.

4. Ministry is a difficult work that will require all of who you are—your strengths and your woundedness—with much of it being

lonely and unglamorous, rather than public and praiseworthy. If you are willing to drink from the same cup as Jesus, if you are open to leaning on him for your strength and direction, the irony is… you might find the vocation of ministry to be a source of great joy and purpose and meaning.

Church leadership is an odd and wondrous calling—and while it may not be the only place that God calls people to spiritual service, it is an important vocation that God is still graciously using to come alongside God's people and bring healing to the world. Thanks be to God, for all those who are called in this way.

www.discoverment.org

Questions for Reflection:

Who are the church leaders who have inspired you or come alongside you in meaningful ways? Who are some lay people (unofficial church leaders) who have informed and supported your spiritual life? What do they have in common? What is unique about their positioning and ability to speak spiritual truths into your life?

What do you imagine is odd about church leadership? What do you imagine might be wondrous about it? What do you think might change about church leadership over the course of your lifetime?

Like many other prominent positions of trust, church leadership has been decimated in recent years by news of scandals and abuse of power. Why do you think the moral failings of church leaders hurt so much?

With all our complaints and critiques of religious institutions, they are still a context where God does show up. What does God possibly see in church institutions? What might God grieve or lament about them? How do you think institutions or systems or structures change and renew themselves? Is there a piece of that work that feels like it's yours?

www.discoverment.org

****

MY JOURNEY TOWARDS MINISTRY
by Tianna Gocan

By the time I was in my second-last year of my undergrad, I had it all figured out, and I mean a detailed 5 year plan figured out. After graduation, I'd get engaged and start my Master's in Science.

Well, God decided to throw a wrench in that 5 year plan. Two years later, I'm not engaged and I'm not starting my Masters. Instead, I'm now discerning the call to become an ordained minister in the Anglican Church of Canada.

Earlier this year, I was wondering what path God was calling me towards because, frankly, my options for my MSc were non-existent. I chose a city, did my research, and sent emails to prospective supervisors, but nothing further came of it. Either they didn't have funding, or they had already accepted someone else. It felt like God was literally slamming the door to this path right in front of my face.

Around the same time, I went on a Discoverment retreat, and while I was there, I was challenged to think about what doors God had open for me. I was reminded of the time when I had an old friend (who is also a minister) tell me that he thought the Spirit might be calling me to ordained ministry. I was also in the middle of taking a few New Testament courses, which I found to be really interesting. The more I thought about it, the more this path made sense to me. I love God, I find theology fascinating, and I'm a natural-born leader.

Since the retreat, the discernment process has been an exciting journey full of unknowns. I didn't grow up Anglican, so the process of discerning the call to become a priest is completely new to me, and I'm slowly discovering what it fully entails. I've also told the rector of my parish that I've been feeling this calling. He's been the main person behind the scenes who has helped kickstart my discernment journey. I am so glad that I reached out to him when I was starting this, and I would recommend anyone else do the same. At the beginning of this journey, he gave me some great advice. He told me to pay attention to where my interests lie, to be in tune and honest with myself, and to be open to the signs that the Lord is giving me. These skills take a lot of practice and reflection, but they have given me clarity and reassurance that this is what God has called me to do.

Now, I won't lie, it was downright terrifying to think about this at first. The Bible is full of stories of people who were called to do God's work and were scared, had doubts or even tried to run away from the path that God had made for them. Some examples that come to mind are Moses, Jonah and even Jesus Himself in the garden of Gethsemane saying "My Father, if it is possible, may this cup be taken from me." (Matthew 26:39). However, I find comfort in the fact that, at the end of their stories, they found their way to their calling. This unwavering faith that God has a plan for me and my life is what gives me the courage to keep going deeper into my discernment journey, even when I can't always see the light at the end of the tunnel.

I think what has helped me the most on this journey has been to be aware of my thoughts, my interests, and, most importantly to where the Lord is leading me during this season of my life.

www.discoverment.org

MY DISCOVERMENT JOURNEY: WHAT AM I CALLED TO DO?

Use this space to journal about any feelings, questions, or discoverments that came to you as you considered your vocation in this section.

My Daily Discoverment

www.discoverment.org

How do I make decisions?

Discerning between different opportunities
Days 28 – 36

My Daily Discovermeant

✳✳✳✳✳✳✳✳✳✳✳✳✳✳✳✳✳✳✳✳✳✳✳✳✳✳✳✳✳✳✳✳

SET YOUR INTENTION: HOW DO I MAKE DECISIONS?

In this fifth section of reflections, I want to invite you to consider the way in which you make decisions. We'll explore how we identify and decide between the various opportunities that open up to us, and how we respond when opportunities don't develop. We'll engage some of the tools that our Christian tradition offers us for wise decision-making, and we'll consider some of the different emotions we sometimes feel as we take our first tentative steps in a chosen direction.

There's a lot riding on the decisions we make each day. The decisions we make are the building blocks of the life we end up living. There is a whole lot in life that we don't get to choose, which means that the things we can decide are precious, and worth engaging with intentionality and faithfulness. But perhaps there's also some freedom embedded in our relationship with God, and maybe a little joy to be discovered on the way.

Consider:

- What are some of the decisions that have shaped you into who you are today?
- How do you typically approach, make, and live with your decisions? How do you feel about your decision-making process?
- How does your understanding of God, yourself, God's activity, and your own vocation inform your decision-making?

Let's Pray:

God of wisdom, grant me the perspective to view my decisions as you do, as opportunities to partner with you in your healing work. Give me a discerning heart and a listening ear, so I may hear your call amid all the opportunities before me. I trust that you want the best for me and for the world, so journey with me and equip me, through your Spirit. Amen.

www.discoverment.org

****

DAY 28

How to Pray

Ask and it will be given to you; seek and you will find; knock and the door will be opened to you.

For everyone who asks receives; the one who seeks finds;

and to the one who knocks, the door will be opened.

Luke 11:9b-10 (NIV)

I'm not a particularly argumentative person. The Enneagram tests I've done say that I'm a 9, the Peacemaker, so avoiding conflict is sort of my thing.

I don't argue often with the people in my life, but when I do it's usually because I haven't articulated a need or expectation in a way that the other person could hear. It might be as simple as some communication about a task that needs doing and how it ought to be done. Or it could be as complex as navigating the emotional baggage we all carry from our families of origin. Many times when I look back and untangle the various levels of misunderstanding I sometimes fall into, in there somewhere is a failure to express a need and ask for what we want.

Sometimes our relationship with God feels that way too.

When we are discerning our vocations and making decisions about the daily life of faith, it is important that we listen for God's voice, but it's also important that we learn to ask for what we need. Sometimes our prayer life isn't what it could be, because we don't ask God to respond to us in our times of need and decision-making.

But what should we ask God for, especially in our times of decision-making?

Sometimes, when we talk to people at church about our decision-making, they ask us if we have prayed about it. In my experience, however, simply praying that God might serve up solutions and do the work for me, hasn't been very fruitful. The best discernment prayers, I've found, aren't about gimme gimme gimme, as if God were some kind of direction-giving vending machine or magic 8-ball. Instead, the best discernment prayers I know ask God to shape my character to be more like Christ.

As you lead a discerning life, try asking God some of the following in your prayer times.

Pray, help me to see what is true. As you listen to the various voices around you and within you, as you imagine the possible outcomes that lay before you, ask God to help you distinguish what is true from what isn't. Truth can be a bit humbling. Truth can be counter-cultural and risky. Truth can require embracing an entirely new perspective. Truth can often require dismantling and unlearning things; it may feel like a step backwards instead of progress. But ultimately, God's truth roots us in love—for ourselves and for others and for all Creation—and is the freedom we need to flourish and participate in God's healing work.

Pray, shape my desires to be like yours. Scripture tells us that God longs to give us the desires of our hearts (Psalm 37:4). We are shaped by the things we desire, and the things we desire are shaped by the liturgies, the stories, the habits we immerse ourselves in. Prayer is an opportunity to realign our desires with the desires of God. If all we are drawn to in an opportunity is the security it provides and the power it gives me, I likely need to realign my desires with God's.

Pray, increase my faith and help me to trust in your presence. There is no certainty about the outcomes of any of our decisions. The only certainty that exists is that of God's character and the assurance of God's presence. Even if we walk through the most difficult valley and are surrounded by problems and enemies, as described in Psalm 23, we need fear no evil—God still sets before us a feast we can share. Let us be certain in who God is and trust in God's presence with us, instead of banking on the outcomes of any path we follow.

I'm often not sure if my prayers have any effect on the world. But I do know that when I pray—when I try to be honest and loving and open with God—I myself am changed. And it's this changed, prayerful me that I trust with my life and my decisions, more than the version of me who tries to do everything on my own.

Jesus taught us that the one who asks, receives. The one who seeks, finds. And the one who knocks, to them the door will be opened (Matthew 7:8). As we begin to make decisions that will shape our lives and our communities, may we learn to "pray without ceasing" and be formed by our experiences with God.

Questions for Reflection:

What is your prayer life like these days? How has it changed since you were a child? How might it need to evolve as you begin making and living into some big, life decisions? What prevents you from praying boldly and asking God for what you need?

Some corners of Christianity practice a "name it and claim it" form of prayer life—sometimes called the Prosperity Gospel. The thinking is, if you have enough faith and speak it into the world, God will give you what you desire—opportunities, wealth, reputation and more! How is this kind of prayer life different from what Jesus describes in Luke 11:9-10? What are some of the pitfalls or potential abuses of a "gimme gimme" prayer life?

Thomas Merton was a Catholic contemplative of the 20th century. One of his more famous prayers begins with a powerful admission of being lost and confused (Merton, p. 79). Look up the Merton Prayer online. Where do you see, within the Merton Prayer, the three "asks" suggested in our reflection today? What part of the his prayer resonates most with you? Try writing your own prayer that articulates the three "asks" mentioned in this reflection.

How might a well-practiced, mature prayer life aid in the task of decision-making? How do you hope your prayer life might shape you as a follower of Jesus? What other "asks" do you think you might raise before God as you discern your way forward?

My Daily Discoverment

DAY 29

Discernment and Decision-Making

Thus says the LORD: Stand at the crossroads, and look, and ask for the ancient paths, where the good way lies; and walk in it, and find rest for your souls.

Jeremiah 6:16

When our children were little, we had a stretch of a couple of years where both of our kids wanted Harry Potter themed birthday parties. My amazing and imaginative wife would decorate our living room to look just like Hogwarts, with fake cobwebs and battery-operated candles hanging from the ceiling, and creepy portraits of people whose eyes seemed to follow you. She'd buy frog-shaped chocolates, and candy apples, and the tricky little jelly beans that sometimes tasted delicious like butterscotch and cotton candy, and sometimes tasted gross like ear wax or roadkill. There were games and loot bags and birthday cake and gifts—all decked out in the Harry Potter theme. My wife went all out for those birthday parties, and our kids loved it.

My role at these parties was to take pictures (so very many pictures!) and be the voice of the Sorting Hat. If you've never read the Harry Potter books, the Sorting Hat is a magical piece of pointy headwear that searches the character of incoming Hogwarts students and separates them into their school houses. We had a replica Sorting Hat for our parties, which each party goer would take a turn donning while they sat on a special chair in our living room. Thankfully nobody gifted us with head lice! From the next room over, when I got the signal, I would use my big loud preacher voice to pontificate about the various virtues and deficiencies of each of our children's friends. After much giggling, and a few exaggerated misdirections, I would assign each of the children to Gryffindor, so they could all be in the same house together and have fun. It was a birthday party after all, not a job interview.

In the book *Harry Potter and the Chamber of Secrets*, there is a point towards the end where Harry is second guessing the Sorting Hat's decision to put him in Gryffindor. Harry has learned he possesses some rare abilities that put him more in touch with the troubling legacy of Slytherin than he initially imagined. The wise headmaster Dumbledore reassures Harry that it is indeed our choices, not our abilities, that reveal who we truly are (Rowling, p. 352). Harry's desire to be in Gryffindor, and the decisions he made since embracing the opportunity to be in that house, showed that he truly belonged and affirmed the Sorting Hat's pronouncement over him.

Our choices—the big, consequential, life changing ones and the little every day ones that accumulate to make up a life—reveal to us who we really are and shape who we are becoming. It's as true in the world of Harry Potter as it is in real life.

Elizabeth Liebert, in her book *The Way of Discernment: Spiritual Practices for Decision-Making*, writes:

> *Through our choices, we can become the person God is calling us to be. Because our decisions are so central to our identity as persons and as Christians, we can look to the Christian tradition for help in the process of decision making. That help is called discernment.* (Liebert, p.7)

Discernment is the practice of faithful decision making. It becomes our task whenever we are forced to choose between different, but comparably persuasive, opportunities. Discernment is not something we leave to coin tosses or chance. It is work; people wrestle with their decisions. Discernment requires seeking out and coaxing forth truth and different points of view. It requires imagination, weighing the differences between possible ways forward, and stepping out in faith towards a single option, knowing full well that nothing is guaranteed and no outcome can ever be 100% sure. Discerning takes place when we approach our decisions with care and our whole selves—for we are called to be good stewards of our choices.

Above all, discernment involves sorting through the opportunities that present themselves to us, and determining where we hear God's call being reflected back to us, and where we don't. Discernment requires us to continue listening for God's voice through the spiritual practices we engage, the shared input of our community, and the sense of vocation that God gifts us with. As we listen, may we hear anew the invitation to participate in God's healing work, and God's pronouncement of belovedness over us.

Just as we are formed by the decisions we make, so too is the world shaped by us when we listen and discern with—as we decide and eventually work alongside—God in the healing of Creation.

Questions for Reflection:

How do you feel about the idea that we are shaped by the decisions we make? What are some decisions you've made that have been particularly formative? What aspects of your identity did you have no choice over at all? How do those two things—our decisions and the things we have no agency in—work together to form you into who God is calling you to be?

Write about a decision you had to make that was particularly difficult. What were the opportunities that were open to you? How did you sort through and differentiate between them? What was the process by which you arrived at a decision? What feelings do you have now, as you look back on that process?

My Daily Discoverment

Discernment comes from the Latin word that means to discriminate. We usually think of discrimination as a negative thing. In what ways might we need to reimagine the word "discriminate" in order to shine a positive light on our decision making?

Does who you are—including how you are wired and gifted—shape how you go about making decisions? What aspects of your identity are helpful for careful discernment? Which aspects of your identity are challenges to careful discernment?

www.discoverment.org

✳✳✳✳✳✳✳✳✳✳✳✳✳✳✳✳✳✳✳✳✳✳✳✳✳✳✳✳✳✳✳✳✳

DECISION PARTNERS
by Andrea Hyde

I remember quite clearly the pressure to become partnered at an early age.

According to the voices around me, it was important to: get a boyfriend in elementary school (even if there was no one I was interested in), and then to keep a boyfriend (even if he wasn't the right fit for me), and eventually to marry that boyfriend (even if I wasn't ready). I watched plenty of sitcoms that made use of the "will they/won't they" trope, and romantic comedies that made clear a view that life was truly better when you found "the One". In university it seemed I was constantly surrounded by couples. I internalized the romantic relationship as being the be all and end all of life as a young adult. When my younger cousin married while I was in my second year of university I remember thinking, "When will I meet my Prince Charming?"

Well, I did meet my future husband in my final year of university—you've been reading his reflections throughout most of this workbook. But I'm not sure it exactly matched my fairytale expectations. We started as friends, and eventually decided we were "official" a few months later. Before I knew it, I was in a relationship and wondering if this is what God had planned for me. I was no longer just thinking about my plans and my future, but reframing things around our plans and our future.

It was equally exciting and frustrating as I learned to communicate my thoughts and feelings with Andrew, and grew to understand his thoughts and feelings too. To be honest, communication is something we still find a worthwhile but difficult challenge many years into our marriage. And now that we have children, there are more perspectives to take into account, more voices to be heard, as we make decisions together. It takes time, it takes patience, and it takes humility as we learn from each other. Listening is hard work—especially when we listen to really understand each other and discern together, rather than to convince each another or win arguments.

My Daily Discoverment

When I was single (that is, before meeting Andrew), I was the one that made all of the decisions regarding my education, where I was going to live and with whom, how I was going to pay all of my bills, and what job I would land. Prayer was a big part of making those decisions. I would read my Bible in the mornings, journal, and meditate asking God for guidance. In addition, I would discuss my options with friends and family members who provided their wisdom on the major life decisions I faced. However, ultimately the decisions were up to me.

Once Andrew and I were married, decision-making became a bit more complicated, but ultimately led us to become closer to one another as we worked through (and prayed through) our various disagreements and confusion together. Most times, we've been able to make a decision that resulted in both of us feeling heard and valued. The more difficult decisions require us to be gracious with each other as we asked really good questions, about our assumptions, hopes, points of view and why they're so important to us. Fortunately (so far) we've found ways to navigate those more challenging discussions, even when the decisions were difficult.

Decision making for me has always been a challenge. The gift of my partnership with God, my husband and children, as well as my supportive community of family and friends have really helped me grow in this area. Have I made mistakes? Absolutely! Have I grown from those mistakes? I sure hope so. Am I thankful to have a partner for decision-making? Usually.

Not everyone is called to live a married life or to start a family. There are all sorts of ways that people experience loving relationships that challenge and support us in equal measures. And there are just as many ways to navigate the various challenges and demands those relationships place on your decisions.

Whatever relationships God leads you into, may your decision making be guided by love, open communication, and prayer. And may you find the support you need when you need it, without all the unnecessary expectations of others.

www.discoverment.org

****

DAY 30

Recognizing Opportunity

> Some went out on the sea in ships; they were merchants on the mighty waters… They mounted up to the heavens and went down to the depths; in their peril their courage melted away. They reeled and staggered like drunkards; they were at their wits' end. Then they cried out to the LORD in their trouble, and he brought them out of their distress. He stilled the storm to a whisper; the waves of the sea were hushed. They were glad when it grew calm, and he guided them to their desired haven.
>
> Psalm 107:23-30

Flying in an airplane is not my favourite thing in the world. I'm not super comfortable with heights, and any kind of turbulence sends me quivering. People who know me have suggested that it's a control issue, and if I were allowed to be up in the cockpit flying the plane, I'd probably be fine—even if everyone else would be justifiably nervous.

My anxiety around flying was especially heightened one spring, when I was leading a group of young adults on an exposure and learning trip with some of our church partners in Central America. Flying south from Canada, we had to change planes in Miami, and as we came in to land, a nasty storm was swirling in from the Atlantic Ocean. We passed once by the airport, then twice by the airport, each time unable to land because of high winds and torrential downpours. As we circled around Miami again, the airplane was tossed up and down like a dice in the canister of a Yahtzee game. On the third approach, we ricocheted our way down towards the tarmac. The sudden drop of altitude and the constant buffeting of the wind had me on the brink of vomiting. I prayed. I assessed my life. And then we bounced our way to a hard landing and sloshed our way down the runway. The lights came on, and all the young adults I was accompanying had giant smiles on their faces. I was as pale as a ghost.

Whether you are landing on the ground at an airport, or sailing into safe harbour from rough seas, there is a wonderful feeling that comes over you when you finally make landfall. It feels a little like home. We can breathe easier, having arrived safe at our destination.

Similarly, there can be a sense of relief and excitement and expectant motivation when our vocational calling finally finds expression, by landing in some real life opportunity. Until we connect with an opportunity, a setting in which we can live out the work we feel called to, our vocation is simply an idea, an aspiration, a hope, or a plan.

The word opportunity comes from the Latin phrase *ob portum veniens*, which refers to a favourable wind blowing ships into safe harbour. An opportunity, therefore, is our chance to land and find grounding for our lofty ideas about who we are and what we are called to do. An opportunity puts flesh onto the framework of our vocational aspirations. An opportunity incarnates and makes real and tests the things we believe about ourselves and our purpose in life. An opportunity is literally where the rubber meets the road, when it comes to pursuing our vocational calling.

You might think of yourself as having a calling towards educating others. You might sense within yourself a desire and the gifts to teach, you might be passionately convinced of the need for teachers in the world, but until you have an opportunity to do so, and someone is willing to be your pupil, your vocation is simply an idea.

You might think of yourself as having a calling to art, or advocacy, or ministry, or medicine, but until you have an opportunity to pursue that calling, your vocation remains an abstraction.

Of course, some opportunities align with our sense of vocation better than others. Some opportunities aren't worth pursuing. Some opportunities are stepping stones to other opportunities. Some opportunities feel less like a final destination and more like a harbour that is safe-enough-for-now.

What each opportunity requires is a response. If the response is no, then stay out at sea and wait for more favourable winds. If the response is yes, then raise your sails, catch hold of the wind, and make for port. Find landing for your sense of God's call, and get to work until God puts some other calling or a better opportunity before you.

There's an old phrase that some people use, to express their excitement at good fortune: "my ship has finally come in." There's also an old Christmas carol that expresses similar joy at the news of the birth of Christ—I saw three ships come sailing in, on Christmas Day in the morning. Both harken back to a time when merchant ships represented vast fortunes out at sea and the uncertainty and precariousness of those riches until they came into harbour. Seeing your ship come into port meant good news and the realization of your hopes, whether they be commercial or spiritual.

Likewise, your Creator has a lot invested in your vocational calling. There are great hopes for the healing of the world riding on your ability to identify your calling and find opportunities to live out your vocation. May we therefore find favourable winds that bring us safely to port; may we find the opportunities we need to participate in the work God has prepared for us.

Questions for Reflection:

What does it mean to be spiritually grounded?

We sometimes refer to Jesus as the Word made flesh. We also use the word incarnational when we talk about God taking on human form and living in our real world. Why do you think it is important for our vocational life to find expression in the real world? Which is more important, how we think about our calling or how we live it? What might it mean to live an incarnational faith?

Write about an opportunity—for school, or work, or something similar—that presented itself to you, and you said no. What was your reasoning? How did you come to your decision? What did you feel during and after your decision-making process? Similarly, write about an opportunity, where you responded with a reluctant or temporary yes. Then write about an opportunity, where your response was an emphatic yes.

People sometimes use the phrase "a bird in the hand is worth two in the bush" to describe the value of actuality over potentiality. Do you agree? Is something that's real but less ideal better than something that's uncertain but more ideal? How might your response shape your approach to the different opportunities that come your way?

My Daily Discoverment

****

A DIFFICULT DECISION
by Kimberly Ivany

At the end of April, 2015, I was finishing a contract at the Canadian Broadcasting Corporation (CBC). I graduated from Ryerson University in Toronto with a bachelor of journalism in 2012 and had been working on a casual basis with the CBC since then.

For about a year, however, I had been feeling a strong pull toward ministry. My upbringing surely affected the blossoming of this heart tug—my dad had been a United Church minister for more than two decades—but, more importantly, my independent journey into adulthood had opened my eyes to God's presence in personal and tangible ways.

I was at a discernment retreat in February when I decided to make 2015 a year where I would fully allow God to move in my life. I wanted to learn how to surrender, in the process of searching for what I'm meant to be doing.

I had nothing concrete lined up work-wise when the CBC project came to a close, but I did have a three-week trip to Europe planned.

At this particular fork in the road, my cousin made an appearance.

Jenn mentored me through my teenage years and, at the time, was a Salvation Army officer in British Columbia. We hadn't spoken in a while when she sent me an e-mail with the application for a year-long placement with The Salvation Army's International Social Justice Commission in New York.

In response to a divine conviction in her heart that I should be working there, Jenn called the director to tell him about my work experience.

The night before I left for Europe, she called me and said, "I spoke with the director. If you're up for this, he is willing to offer you a short-term position for the summer."

I immediately said yes, sent my resumé and the placement was confirmed.

When I got home at the end of May, however, my preparation for this imminent cross-border adventure was shaken when I got a call from a producer at the CBC's *The Fifth Estate*.

He was looking for an associate producer for a documentary for six months. Not only that, it would be a co-production with *Frontline*—the United States' equivalent to *The Fifth Estate*.

I expressed my deep interest at the same time as telling the producer about my New York opportunity with the Salvation Army. We both agreed I would take a few days to think about it.

Those days were nothing short of an inner tug of war, marking what was the hardest decision I had to make up to that point.

I spent the week in ceaseless thought, making endless pros and cons for both. How could a budding journalist say no to *The Fifth Estate* and *Frontline*? I called Jenn. I spoke with friends and family. I talked to God. It was His voice that came through the loudest.

The decision finally anchored itself in my gut when I read this piece of scripture, titled The Solution is Life on God's Terms: "Anyone, of course, who has not welcomed this invisible, but clearly present God… won't know what we're talking about. But you who welcome him… you yourself experience life on God's terms… So don't you see that we don't owe this old do-it-yourself life one red cent. There's nothing in it for us, nothing at all. The best thing to do is give it a proper burial and get on with your new life. God's spirit beckons. There are things to do and places to go!" (Romans 8:9-14 MSG).

And so, I went to New York, trusting that God would use this choice for something great.

The neon of Times Square and the energy of Midtown East where I lived grasped all my attention in the first few days before I found my own rhythm, working in the area of communications for the ISJC.

My first task for the ISJC was to write a research paper analyzing communication from a theological perspective. I then extracted those discoveries to develop a web strategy and used it to re-vamp the ISJC website.

I participated in dialogue during meetings and side events at the United Nations surrounding intergovernmental negotiations on the UN's post-2015 agenda.

Every Thursday, my roommate/fellow intern and I led a Bible study at a Salvation Army rehab centre in Manhattan. This was my first experience ever leading a study.

I also had the opportunity to lead devotions at the United Nations Church Centre, preaching my first real sermon.

Though there were high times, those moments were equally matched with deep valleys.

My decision to say no to the CBC, for one, came with residual anxiety about where my life was heading and I often got stuck in visions of "what ifs," particularly at the start of the summer.

But as gold is refined through fire, it was through those patches of doubt that God spoke to me the most. As much as that summer's purpose was to contribute to the work of the ISJC, it was also a season of intense spiritual amplification.

I learned that summer what it means to trust.

And I learned the truth about my relationship with God.

As much as we long for God, so too does She long for us. Without doing a thing, we are unconditionally and deeply loved by a being who designed us with a desire to chase after Her. Not just to reach the end goal, but in the every day.

In the constant flow of New York City, I learned that when we make time and space for God to move, She truly does—in ways that I could not even anticipate.

www.discoverment.org

✱✱✱✱✱✱✱✱✱✱✱✱✱✱✱✱✱✱✱✱✱✱✱✱✱✱✱✱✱✱✱✱

DAY 31

The Sunlight of Opportunity

Is not this the kind of fasting I have chosen: to loose the chains of injustice and untie the cords of the yoke, to set the oppressed free and break every yoke?

Isaiah 58:6 (NIV)

In our backyard, we have a little garden patch that receives a lot of sunlight. In it, I can grow all sorts of good things—tomatoes and cucumbers, zucchini and beans—with relative ease. Having access to plentiful sunlight is a huge benefit for this part of our garden.

We have another little garden patch as well, in an area that is covered by shade for most of the day. I tried growing tomatoes in this setting, but it didn't work. I tried growing beans there too, but they didn't take. The only thing I can grow there, it seems, is kale. Long, leafy, bitter, resilient kale. I don't even particularly like kale, but I grow it because it's the only option available to me in this part of the garden. If only I could let a little more sunlight in my yard, maybe prune back some of the big shady trees or raise up this particular garden a little, I wouldn't have to eat yucky old kale all summer. Being cut off from the sunlight really limits what is possible in this part of our world.

In 1968, just a few months before his death, Rev. Dr. Martin Luther King Jr. gave a speech titled "The Other America." In it, he paints a picture of two very different realities that exist in our society. One is marked by prosperity, whiteness, and "the sunlight of opportunity" (King). People in this America do not lack for an abundance of choice—be it in education, politics, housing, careers, the church, or any other field of society.

In the other America, however, a potent mixture of poverty and prejudice, stigma and racial oppression, quashes down the population's hope, and limits the opportunities available to people. Lack of jobs, poor housing, inadequate schools, and myriad other ailments are chronic occurrences here—symptoms of an unjust and imbalanced society. This other America, then and now, is an all too common experience for Black and Indigenous communities, People of Colour, and other marginalized peoples in our world.

For those of us living in the sunlight of opportunity—if we are to make sense of the opportunities that lay before us, to sort through them, and to open ourselves to God's call within them—we have a responsibility to begin our discernment by interrogating these opportunities and asking hard questions of them.

- How did these opportunities come to present themselves to us?
- What structures caused them to be? What systems do they uphold?
- Why might these opportunities be opening up to me and not someone else?
- What status quo is maintained by my entering into this opportunity?
- What status quo might be challenged if I do so thoughtfully and intentionally?
- What opportunities are better taken up by others and how might I use my power, my voice, to facilitate that?

In our eagerness and hurry to find an opportunity that aligns with our vocation, in our desperation to ground our sense of self and guide our work, we cannot lose sight of the new reality God is trying to create—a single reality, for all people, marked by justice and wholeness for all. Nor can we continue to pretend we don't benefit from the divisions that exist in the status quo.

One of the biggest lies in our society today, is the idea that we earn the opportunities that open up to us, that hard work correlates to the number of options available to us. We do not live in a meritocracy. It takes more work, more effort, more patience and restraint to be poor and oppressed than it will ever take to discern life in the sunlight of opportunity. Truthfully, we live in a world with much brokenness, where the sins of racism, white supremacy, and other forms of prejudice have infected the systems and institutions that open up opportunities for us and have skewed our sense of hard work and entitlement. We must reject the myth of meritocracy, and other lies like it, that entrench and maintain the two realities described by Dr. King.

Does that sound like more than you bargained for? Nobody said living for Jesus was going to be easy. Choices that seem harmless and innocuous on the surface often uphold some pretty nasty systems in our world. It is our shared responsibility to dismantle the systems that oppress some for the benefit of others. We do that, in part, by interrogating our opportunities, decision by decision, over the course of our whole lives—by planting seeds of justice that might only bear fruit generations from now.

Questions for Reflection:

Where do you experience a wealth of opportunity? What are some of the barriers to opportunity you experience? What results when people experience a lack of opportunity over a lifetime? What surfaces within you as you imagine your level of opportunity alongside others'?

Where do you see evidence of the two realities that Dr. King describes? What motivates people to deny or hide from this reality?

Racial justice advocates today teach it is not enough to simply be non-racist; people in society have a responsibility to become anti-racist. As you think of the opportunities before you, how might you engage them in a way that actively challenges the status quo, instead of simply waiting for change to happen?

Dr. King gave his life for the cause of justice. How do you sense God calling you to sacrifice things like comfort and safety in service of God's mission? What inspires and encourages you as you pursue the dangers of this work?

My Daily Discoverment

✳✳✳✳✳✳✳✳✳✳✳✳✳✳✳✳✳✳✳✳✳✳✳✳✳✳✳✳✳✳✳

CALLED TO SOLIDARITY
by Ben Reid-Howells

I grew up in a culture of typical Christian charity. Each year, I looked forward to serving dinner to the homeless on Christmas Eve from my local church hall. I went to Central America with my church on trips during high school, to help build houses and learn about social justice.

But what does it mean to follow the path of Jesus and move beyond charity, to solidarity?

In the words of Indigenous artist, activist and academic Lilla Watson, "If you have come here to help me, you are wasting your time. But if you have come because your liberation is bound up with mine, then let us work together" (Watson).

For me, real justice does not mean charity. It does not mean giving to the poor, but taking a look at the systems that are in place that create and maintain the rich and the poor. It means looking at these systems, and working together to dismantle them.

Jesus was good at this. He challenged the connected systems of oppression around him. From the patriarchal culture he lived in, to the power hungry religious authorities. From the capitalist marketplace, to the occupying colonial Roman government.

On my own journey from handing out food to the poor, to building healing centres with Indigenous nations, I have asked myself… "What is the difference between charity and solidarity?"

If charity is "benevolence for the poor"—which can indeed reinforce the same systems that keep some meek enough to beg and others powerful enough to give—solidarity means interdependent, complete, entire, a communion of interests and mutual responsibility.

And herein lies the difference. We are not called to serve others. We are called to work together for our collective liberation. Not to engage in outreach to "vulnerable communities," but to reach inwards, to our own shared humanity—together oppressed and together yearning for wholeness.

In my own journey, I realize that I am not called to charity, but to solidarity.

The *missio dei* or mission of God is not to evangelize, to be missionaries. The mission we have as followers of the teachings of Jesus is to extract ourselves from the violent systems around us and to work together with all children of Creation, human and non-human, to heal.

In my path from charity to solidarity work I often ask myself, what does it mean for ME to engage in solidarity work?

As a white settler in "Canada," I feel called to join the efforts of those who are challenging the systems of violence in this country: our extractivist industries—oil and gas, and other natural resources—that rely on the displacement of Indigenous peoples from their land; our migrant detention centres and prisons, which incarcerate refugees like Mary and Joseph and criminalize people of colour. I feel called to challenge gender-based violence, and socially accepted expressions of racism in my friend-group and workplace.

For me, when I heed the call of God, this call to solidarity, I feel a healing from a sense of separation. I feel connected to Christ, to the Holy Spirit, and indeed to all those working towards liberation around the world, regardless of the name they give to the Divine.

DAY 32

Wisdom and Creativity

> Forget the former things; do not dwell on the past.
> See, I am doing a new thing! Now it springs up;
> do you not perceive it? I am making a way in
> the wilderness and streams in the wasteland.
>
> Isaiah 43:18-19 (NIV)

When I was younger, there were only a handful of TV stations, and cartoons were only aired on Saturday mornings. Consequently, I watched a lot of game shows. One of the most popular game shows in my childhood drew contestants from a crowd of outlandishly costumed audience members, who would participate in a variety of games of skill and chance, based loosely on their consumer savvy. In reality, it was a platform for corporations to display and promote their products to gullible contestants and consumers at home.

Each episode culminated with an opportunity for contestants to trade away their prizes for what was hiding behind Door #1, Door #2, or Door #3. One of the doors would be hiding the day's grand prize, while the other two hid either a modest prize or a joke. The drama behind making the right choice was palpable each time you watched it.

Wisdom is one's capacity for making good decisions. You may remember that King Solomon, when asked to name what he most desired from God, asked for wisdom (1 Kings 3). Choosing well and discerning our next step deeper into God's calling, takes wisdom.

Wisdom gathers information before making a decision: it listens to other wise people; it learns from previous experiences; it sees the world as it truly is, rejecting both naive optimism and the haze of despair. Wisdom imagines possible outcomes. It anticipates future benefits and counts future costs—the burdens placed on ourselves, others, and Creation. Wisdom is humble. Wisdom can be developed over time. Wisdom involves the whole person—the intellectual mind, the heart, the body, and the soul. In the book of James, scripture tells us that if we lack wisdom we should ask God for it, and it will be given (James 1:5). Wisdom is required for good discernment.

But there is one aspect of wisdom that is often overlooked. Wisdom is also creative. Wisdom blows open our scope of what is possible. Wisdom expands our sense of the opportunities before us.

In the book of Proverbs, the fruit of wisdom is on display in manageable bite-sized form. There are loads of pithy sayings that people like to quote and haul out to guide their discernment. But towards the beginning of Proverbs, wisdom takes the symbolic form of a person—Lady Wisdom—who waits for us, accompanies us, and guides us as we discern our way through life.

In Proverbs 8—a passage that mirrors the description of Jesus in John, chapter 1—we are invited to imagine Lady Wisdom being right beside God in the act of Creation. "The LORD created me at the beginning of his work," she tells us, "the first of his acts of long ago… when he marked out the foundations of the earth, then I was beside him, like a master worker."

Wisdom is creative. Wisdom helped imagine the great diversity of life. Wisdom creates goodness out of nothing. Wisdom is not bound by the limitations of our understanding, or past precedence, or the scarcity with which we imagine the opportunities before us. Wisdom looks at the options that seem most available to us and knows there is a whole world of possibility beyond them. As John Ortberg argues in his book *All the Places to Go*, "Very often the choice isn't Door #1 or Door #2. It's Door #14" (Ortberg, p.124). Sometimes when we feel our options are limited, Wisdom is calling us to create or consider or imagine something new.

When the Israelites were called by God out of slavery and into freedom, they ran into a situation where they assumed their only options were to be drowned in the sea or killed by Pharaoh's army. Wisdom had them turn to God, who opened a new path for them through the Red Sea.

When Mary was called to give birth to the son of God, Joseph assumed his only options were to live with the shame of an unfaithful wife or dismiss her quietly. Wisdom spoke to Joseph and opened up a new path for the Holy Family.

When Paul was in jail and an earthquake opened the door to his jail cell, his followers assumed their options were a life on the run from the

Roman authorities or a life of imprisonment. Wisdom spoke to Paul and together they discerned a new option, whereby the Roman guards were convinced of God's goodness and mercy and grace.

Sometimes Wisdom comes to us like the creativity of an artist. Sometimes Wisdom arrives like the risk-taking courage of an entrepreneur. Wisdom doesn't only appear to us in the careful analysis of the accountant, weighing pro's and con's. Wisdom is felt and imagined and risked, just as much as it is considered, compared and thought through.

Making wise decisions means sorting through the various opportunities that open up to you, but it also means opening ourselves to the creativity of God and the limitless array of possibilities that exist when we are partnered with God in the building of God's kingdom.

Questions for Reflection:

Have you ever considered the opportunities that lie before you and found yourself unimpressed? Have you ever wished there were more options to choose from? What factors in our society work to limit our sense of what is possible? Which of those factors have merit and which ones seem arbitrary or worth challenging?

Write about wisdom. What makes wisdom different from knowledge or intellectualism? Who are the people in your life whom you consider wise? How might they be a resource to you in your own discernment? Have you ever thought to ask God for wisdom? What else might you ask of God to help you in your discernment?

Sometimes we talk about people who chart a new path in life as being trailblazers. Who are the trailblazers that you emulate? What excites you about the prospect of being a trailblazer yourself? What are some of the risks or hazards of charting a new path? In what areas of our society today do we need people to chart new, unconventional courses?

Many churches and charities make funds and resources available for people who want to start something new. Try searching the website of the denomination you belong to. Try asking some of the leaders in your community. What are some of the resources you might use to blaze a new trail in pursuit of your vocational calling?

www.discoverment.org

****

DAY 33

Going Off Script

For surely I know the plans I have for you, says the Lord, plans for your welfare and not for harm, to give you a future with hope.

Jeremiah 29:11

In our community, one of the local churches hosts a community drama program that invites neighbourhood youth to be part of a play. Our son is part of this group, and so we attend their big production every year. One year the play was a murder mystery set in a hotel. Another year, it was a *Breakfast Club* parody, set in a small town high school. For months on end, we get to hear about all the drama that goes into a producing… a drama. Role assignments, bruised egos, unmemorized lines, and personality conflicts. In the weeks leading up to the production, there's always a crunch of emotional struggle and teenage angst. But every year, we are amazed at the end result. From our vantage point, everyone manages to remember their lines, everyone responds to the right cues, and the show goes off without a hitch. The directors might feel otherwise, but as far as we're concerned, they always manage to pull it off.

I have a lot of respect for people who can learn their part and play it well. There are some people who can absorb a script and recite it back verbatim, who can remember all their cues and the blocking assignments given to them. I, on the other hand, can still manage to fumble the Lord's Prayer while leading worship on Sundays.

Scripts are great. The only problem is when people expect life to unfold like one, with everything laid out, line by line, for them. You may know some of these people—good people—who earnestly want to respond to God's call in their life, who want to be obedient to whatever God might have them do, but who are paralyzed the moment they do not sense God giving them a clear next step, or feeding them the next line in their script.

When God is sometimes silent or unclear, they become fearful of making a wrong step or flubbing their next line.

One of the things we like to say in the church is that God has a plan for our lives. We get that from verses like the one listed above, in Jeremiah. We look at gifted young people and declare that God must have plans for them—the evidence is in their equipping. When tragedy or hardship befall us, we sometimes take solace by placing it in some larger plan that is ultimately for our good.

God may have a plan for you, but I don't believe God has a line by line script that you're intended to memorize and follow. God's plan may include callings and invitations, opportunities that open up to us, nudges and important milestones. But it also includes room to breathe, room for exploration, room to respond creatively and even make mistakes. God's plan, I believe, reads less like a script and unfolds more like dramatic improv. Instead of laying it all out explicitly, God sometimes delights in seeing what you come up with yourself.

Some people say that improv is wide open, completely made up, and spontaneous to the point of silliness. But the people who are good at it, who enroll in and put on improvisational workshops, will tell you there is indeed structure to it, and important principles that good improv actors adhere to, to make it seem so effortless and free. Likewise, there is a knack to discerning and creatively engaging God's plan for your life. It involves being rooted in God's story, knowing yourself, listening for God, seeking wisdom, and responding creatively to where you sense God moving in your life.

One of the key principles of good improv is that of "Yes… and…". The "yes" part requires listening for and affirming what your partner is opening up for you. It doesn't try to reject what is offered or shoe-horn some other reality into the scenario. Then the "and" part adds something new to it, perhaps a new twist or possibility, it adds a new layer of complexity or beauty or humour, to which your partner then in their own way responds. Improv requires a creative back and forth, where layers of affirmation and creativity combine to make a compelling story.

Sometimes we expect a script and rigid direction from God, when instead we are invited to partner with God in an improv.

In her book *An Altar in the World*, Barbara Brown Taylor tells the story of a time when she was seeking direction for what to do with her life. Each evening, she would climb out on a dingy old fire escape overlooking her college and pray to God, but receive only silence. After many nights of frustrating prayer, the Divine spoke to her soul, inviting her to do anything she pleased, so long as she belonged to God (Taylor, p. 110).

I too, recall a time when I was deciding which university to attend. The school close to home, the school by the river, the school with the classic old buildings—they each had their virtues and their drawbacks. After much praying to God—and no clear direction emerging—I sensed that God was waiting (no… delighting) to see what I would choose for myself. I was confident that God would walk with me, no matter which path I chose, and that freed me up to make a choice I felt good with.

In 1854, the catholic hymn writer Frederick W. Faber published a collection of praise songs titled *Oratory Hymns*. In that collection, is a little gem of a hymn I recall singing in my youth. Check out a few of the verses…

> *There's a wideness in God's mercy, like the wideness of the sea;*
> *There's a kindness in His justice, which is more than liberty.*
>
> *But we make His love too narrow, by false limits of our own;*
> *And we magnify His strictness with a zeal He will not own.*
>
> *Was there ever kinder shepherd, half so gentle, half so sweet,*
> *As the Saviour who would have us come and gather at His feet? (Faber)*

God has a plan for our lives. Plans for our welfare and a future with hope. But within God's plan there is some wideness, some room for creativity, some space into which God hopes we insert our own imagination, compassion, and love. God does not spell everything out for us or expect us to regurgitate a script.

But make no mistake—God knows where this story is going. Like a kind shepherd, God is gathering us together in justice and mercy and love. Together, we are writing and acting and living, the story of the world's redemption.

Questions for Reflection:

Are you someone who likes to have a script to work from, or do you prefer a lot of room to improvise? What might that say about how you are gifted and the kind of work you might be called towards?

How do you respond to the notion that God has a plan for your life? Is that a helpful and comforting expression, or does it place pressure on you to get it right? The Israelites who heard this word from God, were experiencing a period of exile and captivity. How might this promise be received by people in that context, in ways that differ from (or resonate with) your own? What might a future with hope look like for you?

What is comforting about the idea of God giving us a script for how our life should unfold? What is confining about it? What is exhilarating about the idea of doing improv with God? What is daunting about it?

When Barbara Brown Taylor sensed God inviting her to do anything she pleased, it was followed up by the stipulation of belonging to God. How might belonging to God inform (or release us to make) decisions about what we are called to do?

My Daily Discovermment

****

UNQUALIFIED MIRACLES
by Johannes Chan

The wind blows where it chooses, and you hear the sound of it, but you don't know where it comes from or where it goes. So it is with everyone who is born of the Spirit. (John 3:8)

So I'm in a moment of transition right now, having recently graduated, and still looking for work. The process of finding work, for me is at times one ridden with anxiety, and so I wanted to briefly talk about both the uncertainty and the insignificance I've struggled with as both a student and now a graduate seeking employment.

In 2014, I started studying environmental engineering and international development at the University of Guelph. I had hopes of maybe working for an NGO one day, and grad school seemed like another step I could take towards that goal.

But I soon felt very uncertain and doubtful about what I was doing.

Around the time I was reading a book by Peter Singer called *The Most Good You Can Do*. He briefly argued, in utilitarian terms, that while working at an NGO for a low salary might be noble, it might not be the best way to do the 'most good' possible (Singer). Singer reasoned that you might do "more good" by landing the highest paying job possible (within certain ethical parameters) and donating most of your income to what he considered the most highly 'effective charities' (i.e. donating any income in excess of a typical NGO salary).

Peter Singer's book in some ways shattered my confidence with respect to what I was doing in grad school, which was an attempt to combine engineering and international development. I was also struggling with the fact that I'd maybe never be a competent enough engineer to directly do anything significant about poverty and inequality. I felt like I no longer had a clear way forward, no clear exodus from the type of career trajectory I had grown disillusioned with as an undergraduate student—one preoccupied with the problems of the world's richest 10%.

In Genesis 16, there's a story of a young Egyptian slave girl who runs away from her affliction under Abram and Sarai, and God finds her by a well and asks, "Hagar, slave-girl of Sarai, where have you come from and where are you going?" She said, "I am running away from my mistress Sarai." (Genesis 16:8)

As we continually wonder where the Spirit comes from and to where the Spirit goes in our messy realities, God maybe also wonders, and asks: Where have you come from and where are you going?

There is something seductive about a deterministic certainty. The idea that you can neatly add up things and predictably reach the summation you want.

We may often think of uncertainty, unknowing, and chaos as something to be at best tolerated, to come to terms with—but I think maybe chaos is also a type of miracle, a wide expansive canvas, where the Holy Spirit has creative agency to paint colourfully unexpected brushstrokes in a world of remarkably consistent regularities, that seem to confine us to deterministic equations and predictable outcomes.

The Holy Spirit is not something we control. A difficult concept for an engineering student schooled daily in the practice of learning how to control things.

Engineers interested, for instance, in wind energy make it their business to figure out where the wind comes from and goes to. Wind turbines after all are expensive; they take energy and mined resources to manufacture, transport, construct. We want to make them worthwhile in our imagined world of scarcity.

While the principles behind wind can be thought of in quite simple terms, largely resulting from the Sun's uneven heating of the earth's surface, predicting the wind and the weather can be notoriously difficult.

Edward Lorenz, a pioneering mathematician in 'chaos theory' coined the term the 'butterfly effect,' provocatively suggesting how a butterfly flapping its wings in one continent could create a hurricane in another.

While working on a computational weather model at MIT in the winter of 1961, Lorenz wanted to rerun a simulation, and just copied in the needed values to restart it from the middle, before stepping out for a coffee break. But when he got back, instead of finding what should have been a duplicate of the last simulation output, puzzlingly the plot looked completely different.

He soon figured out he had typed in the initial values to an accuracy of three decimal places rather than six. The difference shouldn't have mattered. Weather data collected to the third decimal place was often considered more than adequate. But this small difference led to a very different outcome. Even in a system of deterministic equations the smallest change could lead to an entirely different result.

Maybe analogously, in a world governed by stable and consistent physical laws of nature, the Holy Spirit emerges in the midst of what we choose to call 'miracles', planted by the smallest of actions from the help of the most unqualified of people.

www.discoverment.org

****

DAY 34

The Overwhelm

For this reason I remind you to rekindle the gift of God that is within you through the laying on of my hands; for God did not give us a spirit of cowardice, but rather a spirit of power and of love and of self-discipline.

2 Timothy 1:6-7

Where I grew up, 19 was the age you had to be to purchase and consume alcohol legally. It was a rite of passage to be able to order your first drink in the pub, to be asked for your ID, and to make your first trip to the Beer Store. This was back in the days in our province, before beer could be purchased in the local grocery or variety store or by ordering an online delivery. You had to go to the one government-run beer store in town—that or the liquor store at the other end of town, which was also run by the government.

My first trip to the Beer Store, I recall, did not go smoothly. I expected it to be like any other store, with displays and coolers and a counter where you'd make your purchase. Instead, I was surprised to enter into a stark, nearly empty cinder block room, with conveyor belts that whirled like the bottoms of roller skates when people brought in their cases of empties. A tiny cash register sat on a stainless steel desk in the corner, where an unenthusiastic clerk mumbled orders into a microphone. Behind her, a dark portal led to a secret back room, and every once in a while a case of beer rolled out of it onto the roller belt for someone to hoist under their arm and carry away.

On the far wall, like a menu stretching from the conveyor belt all the way up to the ceiling, were the listings of all the available beer brands, the case sizes they came in, and the prices. There were lagers and ales and stouts and IPAs, pilsners and porters and ciders galore. Imports, exports, domestics, and microbrews. Six packs, twelve packs, cases of 24 or 28. Tall boys, bottles, stubbies, and kegs. The variety was astounding. Surf boys and construction workers read the beer wall like they were investors reading the stock listings, before making their order with the clerk at the register. I, on the other hand, didn't know what I was looking at. I didn't know what I was looking for. I was overwhelmed, and there was a line beginning to form impatiently behind me. I got flustered, walked out, and had to compose myself before trying again.

There are at least three things that can overwhelm us in the process of decision-making—too many options, the fear of missing out, and the pressure we feel to make the very best choice imaginable.

One of the myths our consumer culture tells us is that more choice is inherently better. Check out the cereal aisle at your local grocery store, or the calendar of degree programs available at your local university. Visit the local mega-church and see all the different kinds of services and programs they make available, or scroll through the number of shows, movies, or series you can watch at any given moment on Netflix. You can even swipe through a dating app and determine, in an instant, a wide selection of people who may (or may not) want to go out on a date with you. We are experiencing an abundance of choice in almost every facet of our lives right now. And it is stressing us out.

This over-abundance of choice filters down to the decisions we make about living out our vocations. Society tells us we can be anything we want. We don't have to be pinned down by others' expectations, the family business, our location, or the needs of our community. If the right opportunity doesn't present itself, you can create it by becoming an entrepreneur or starting your own business. There is a lot of freedom to pursue our callings, but sometimes that freedom creates anxiety.

When we are paralyzed by an over-abundance of choice, we need to become good at saying no and whittling down the field a bit. Jesus told his disciples to let their yes be yes, and their no be no (Matthew 5:37). In today's landscape of unparalleled choice, we are going to have to say no a lot more than we say yes.

But it can be a struggle to say no, because of the fear of missing out. This fear prevents us from embracing the things we've said yes to, so it can hold on to the imaginary outcomes of the things we've said no to. FOMO wonders if the grass might've been greener. FOMO wonders about what might've been. FOMO compares all the hardships and struggles of your yes, to the imaginary benefits held hostage within your no. Fear of missing out is a self-fulfilling prophecy because in wondering what we missed, we end up missing what we chose.

Behind our experience of the fear of missing out, I believe, is a false expectation that we make the very best decision, every single time. What is the best decision, though, for the follower of Jesus? Is it the decision that earns us God's love? We already have that. Is it the decision that produces the most good in the world? I'm not sure that God requires our achievements as much as we'd like to believe.

The best decision, I believe, is the most faithful decision we can muster at any particular moment. A faithful decision does not look for certainty or guarantees. A faithful decision entrusts God to work through our efforts and gives glory to God for the results. A faithful decision is made with God, is open to God, and is dependent upon God to redeem and enliven our efforts and abilities in carrying it out. All God ever asks of us is to take the most faithful step we can for today. "Do not worry about tomorrow," Jesus taught to his disciples, "for tomorrow will bring worries of its own. Today's trouble is enough for today" (Matthew 6:34). Take one little step right now in faith, and once you're in that new place, listen, pray, discern, and decide again. If we can build a life made up of baby steps and faithful discernment, we can trust God with the results.

As we make sense of the choices and opportunities before us, let us not be overwhelmed by our fears or by others' expectations. Let us discern with faith, the opportunities God places before us.

Questions for Reflection:

What are some of the fears you have as you approach the tasks of discernment and decision-making? How do you manage the various fears in your life? What strategies might be helpful for you as you face the fears attached to your discernment?

At some point, too many options or opportunities can be overwhelming. How do you know when you are beginning to feel overwhelmed? What limits might you put around your decision-making to help keep your discernment on track? When you hear the phrase "you can be anything that you want," how do you respond?

www.discoverment.org

Have you ever wrestled with the fear of missing out? What else robs you of the ability to be present in the moment?

What does it mean to have faith? How might taking baby steps in faith differ from the pressure to make the very best decision every single time?

My Daily Discoverment

✳✳✳✳✳✳✳✳✳✳✳✳✳✳✳✳✳✳✳✳✳✳✳✳✳✳✳✳✳✳✳

WALKING A PATH OF PEACE
by Robin McGauley

I walk a labyrinth during the times in my life when the way seems unclear, when I don't know where to turn and I can't decide what path to take.

The labyrinth is a winding path that leads to a centre. Unlike a maze, it has no tricks and no dead ends. It isn't a game or a puzzle. It is a walking meditation. In the labyrinth, you are invited to feel 'found' rather than feel 'lost'. As you walk, the labyrinth provides a space to process whatever is on your mind and, somehow, solutions can surface.

Usually what happens for me when I walk a labyrinth is that I end up understanding myself and my life more deeply or more clearly.

A few years ago, in late fall, I was on retreat with some friends. Outside the cabin we rented was a small labyrinth in the grass. It was covered by a thick layer of fallen leaves.

With the first few steps of walking it I noticed that moving through the leaves was difficult. They were wet and heavy. As I walked, the thought that popped into my head was, "Why am I wadding through this?". A few more shuffles through the layer of heavy leaves and my inner voice said, "Just walk away".

I am someone who likes to follow-through on commitments. I usually always finish what I start.

The idea of walking off the labyrinth after only a few steps was not comfortable for me. I shuffled a little bit farther, but the message persisted… "Just walk away". And then a Biblical story came to me, the one where Jesus instructs the disciples that they are to go out, two by two to spread the good news. He tells them that if they are not welcomed that they are to brush the dust from their sandals and walk away.

I walked off the labyrinth. Then, I asked myself "what was that all about?" Walking the labyrinth is always about pondering the potential lesson of the experience.

After reflecting for a while I realized that walking away was profound for me because I had spent almost a year grieving the loss of a job that I loved. I was carrying a sadness within me about what I had left behind. I was wading through a tangle of emotions that were weighing me down, making it hard for me to move forward. The message to 'walk away' was an invitation to leave the grief behind. This labyrinth walk was the moment I knew that I was being invited to let go of my past and start giving myself more fully to the life that was in front of me.

Sometimes I don't get any definitive answers or messages from walking the labyrinth, but I always feel better as a result of having walked the path and calmed my mind.

You can find more information about labyrinths on the Veriditas website: www.veriditas.org

DAY 35

Catching the Moment

> Besides this, you know what time it is, how it is now the moment for you to wake from sleep. For salvation is nearer to us now than when we became believers;
> the night is far gone, the day is near.
>
> Romans 13:11-12a

When I worked at a summer camp, my favourite night of the week was campout night. Each week, we'd take our campers out into the woods for a night of roasting marshmallows by the fire, star spinning, late night discussions about the big questions of life, and sleeping out under the constellations. Every campout, right after dusk, the fireflies would begin to emerge—slowly, one by one, little blips of light, blinking like satellites in the shadows—and we'd try to catch them in our hands.

If you've ever tried catching a firefly, you'll know it is a process with equal parts waiting, watching, and pouncing, and it's best done with a group of friends. It's a tricky business, full of anticipation, and laughs, and feeling out the opportune moment.

Discerning opportunities can sometimes feel like chasing fireflies. Sometimes there are a lot, sometimes only a few. There is a dance between mystery and revelation and movement, complete with rhythm, timing, and grasping the moment. We talk about the opportune time, because some moments are more rife with opportunity than others.

In scripture we often make a distinction between kairos time and chronos time. Chronos time measures things by years and months and hours and seconds. Chronos time is good for scheduling trains and following recipes and awarding gold medals in the hundred metre dash, but it is not always good at knowing the timeliness of the heart. Someone who feels a lot of pressure to be engaged by the time they graduate college, or to be self-sufficient by a particular age, is dealing in chronos time.

Kairos time is about identifying the moment when something is right. It is about knowing when you are ready for something, recognizing the uniqueness of particular circumstances, or sensing when the moment calls for a particular response. Kairos time is something we discern with our heart, not something we count down to on our watch or our calendar.

In a collection of Henri Nouwen's reflections called *Discernment*, he identifies the need to lean into kairos time by questioning whether it is a time to act, a time to wait, or a time to be led (Nouwen).

Perhaps it is a time to act—a time when you are being called to embody the love of Christ in some kind of meaningful action in the world. Just as getting out of bed is often the hardest decision to make each day, so too can overcoming inertia be the most vital part of our decision-making. As the nautical among us say, it is easier to steer a ship that is moving than one on a windless day. You may find your discernment possibilities open up for you as you take the next, most faith-filled step you can muster.

Perhaps it is a time to wait. The prophet Elijah, while on the run from his adversaries, was led by God to a safe place where he discerned his next steps by waiting on the still small voice of the Divine. Stillness is not laziness or procrastination. Stillness is not nothingness or avoidance. Waiting on the Lord is active, faithful, and attentive. Psalm 27 reminds us that waiting on the Lord can be difficult. "Wait for the Lord," it says. "Be strong and let your heart take courage."

Perhaps it is a time to be led. Oftentimes, when we're discerning the opportunities that lie before us, we assume that God wants to initiate something through us, that God wants us to lead some new endeavour, to be the star of our own stories. But sometimes, God calls us to be an important follower in a project that somebody else is leading. Sometimes we discern a call to a healthy submission, to put our own needs for attention and praise aside, and contribute to a greater good, which is different than apathy or defeatism or being swept along by the conveyor belt of others' expectations.

However you discern the various moments in your life—kairos times of action, waiting, and being led—it is often wise practice to hold your decisions lightly. Holding a decision lightly might mean doing the work to gather data that informs your decision but knowing that our knowledge of a situation is only ever partial. Holding a decision lightly might mean making the best decision you can for the time being, but revisiting it down the road sometime. Holding a decision lightly might mean walking forward in faith and trust, but seeking confirmation of your decision through ongoing prayer, listening, and study of scripture. Holding a decision lightly is not the same thing as being non-committal or casual or lazy about your decision-making. It is the faithful way people make decisions, but leave room for life, knowing that the next new moment requiring discernment and decision is always waiting to reveal itself.

There is life and potential, possibility and mystery, in all the various moments we grasp hold of. So hold each moment gently. Leave room for the Spirit. Appreciate each decision for what it is. And let it go.

www.discoverment.org

Questions for Reflection:

Think about the hopes or expectations you have for how your life will unfold. Which expectations are marked in chronos time? Which hopes are marked in kairos time? What do you notice about the groupings you created? What might change in your world if you measured more things in kairos time?

When have you discerned a moment as a time to act? When have you discerned a time to wait? When you have discerned a time to be led? How did you discern the appropriate response in those moments? How did you know when the moment had changed?

When have you held something—a decision, an assertion, a belief, or a relationship—too tightly? What happened? What loosened your grip?

1 Thessalonians 5:21 encourages us to "test everything" and "hold fast to what is good." Hebrews 10:23 says "Let us hold fast to the confession of our hope without wavering, for he who has promised is faithful." Are there some decisions that we should hold firmly, with conviction? How do you discern what kinds of decisions to hold firmly and which ones to hold loosely?

www.discoverment.org

****

DISCERNMENT ON THE GO
by Alana Martin

I was 16 when I went to Guatemala with a group of fellow teens from my home church in Halifax. We traveled with leaders and met partners from an organization called Breaking the Silence, a Nova Scotia/Guatemala solidarity group. I remember coming back from that trip changed. Something was stirring within me, but I didn't know what yet.

I was 18 when I went to Ecuador with a popular secular project-based adventure organization—trying to help me shift my self-oriented thinking towards others and the world. Something felt really off… but I didn't know what yet and I didn't know how to process it. But I was changed again.

I was 19 when I went to Colombia with The United Church of Canada Youth for Peace initiative. We met our United Church partners and with people who told us stories of courage, hope, loss and pain. It was in those moments and in that trip that I finally stopped to listen to God and hear what God was saying to me. I was being called into ministry, but I didn't yet understand what type or how. I just knew it had something to do with being in those places that had been impacted by war, violence and despair, but being there in partnership and in solidarity to hear stories. Not to fix or bring Western/colonial ways.

I started working with The GO Project that summer and it all came together for me. Not in a neat bow or anything… God rarely wraps this up so perfect for us. It's meant to get messy…

GO Project is a ministry that combines faith and justice in the world. It offers community to young people who are discerning their gifts, passions and dreams with experiences that help us to open our eyes and hearts to the needs in our own communities, giving young people tools to create actionable change.

Learning about GO's "discernment through mission" vision, I realized that I was having all of these life-changing and impactful experiences, without the tools to reflect and then act in just ways. The learning reminds me of a spiral: experience, reflect, act and then back to experience again…

My Daily Discoverment

but not at the same point that we started, because now we are changed. Discernment on the go is all about reflecting while doing—doing while reflection. If we're not reflecting, we're just doing and that can lead to doing harm; and if we're not doing, we're just reflecting which can keep us in our comfort zone. Growth happens outside our comfort zones... and maybe even on the GO! Starting at a new school, entering a new phase of life, or entering the workforce are all examples of major transitions in our lives that need us to stop, reflect, and care for our hearts and souls during the journey. Remember to rest, to practice gratitude, to love yourself and your accomplishments, and to seek guidance from God in the times you need. I hope you can find mentors, resources and peers who will support you through the beautiful journeys you will take.

If you're looking for ways to unpack life changing experiences you've had while acting justly in the world—or are looking to have an experience like that in your journey—explore GO Project's program offering near you. www.thegoproject.ca

www.discoverment.org

****

DAY 36

Decision-making and Failure

Always work enthusiastically for the Lord,

for you know that nothing you do
for the Lord is ever useless.

1 Corinthians 15:58b (NLT)

Have you ever failed a course at school? Have you ever dropped the ball and cost your team the game? Have you ever messed up an important relationship or pinned your hopes onto some direction or scheme or opportunity that didn't work out? Yes? Me too.

We all have our share of failure stories to tell.

Often when we think of our failures, we think of the outcomes, instead of the inputs. We get hung up on results and the fruit of our labour, because that is the metric that society wants to see from us. We want to see start-ups turn profitable. We want to see students who graduate from their programs. We want to see something tangible come from the work we put in. We live in a results-based economy.

When we live vocationally, however—when we align ourselves with God's project and discern faithfully the steps we take in response to God's calling—what we put into our decisions is often just as important as what comes out of it. Things like obedience, faithfulness, compassion, imagination and love—the things we pack into our decision-making—are of real value to God. They show us that God is working to shape who we are, decision by decision, maybe even more than the results of our investments.

In scripture, the prophet Jonah is a classic case of someone who failed Discernment 101. Jonah was a prophet of God. He was gifted with the insight to hear God's voice and speak God's truth to his community. But when Jonah receives God's call to go and preach to the people at Nineveh, he runs the other way. His excuses are numerous. Rationally, there is little chance of success on this mission. Instead of responding to God's call with trust and faithfulness and obedience, Jonah takes matters into his own hands and runs from God's call.

There have been times when I have run from God's call, when what God was asking of me was too difficult or risky or inconvenient to my mind. There have also been times when I have chosen what appeared to be safe and successful, even though I may not have sensed much of the Spirit's call in it.

In those moments of discernment failings, I am grateful for the forgiving and gracious nature of God. I can look at the cross of redemption, deposit my failings, let go of my shame and regrets, and envision a new opportunity to heed God's call in my life. For Jonah, God's grace came in the storm that halted his wayward journey, and the belly of the whale where he discerned anew what God was calling him towards.

I take great comfort in the incompleteness of Jonah's story. He does, eventually, go to Nineveh to do what God asks of him. How many times has my obedience to God looked like a pouty child, mouthing a sarcastic "fine," with an eye roll and a "geesh" for good measure? But at the end of his story, Jonah is still holding onto his arguments about the futility of God's call and direction. Jonah is still imperfect and learning, and God is still patient with him.

We can learn from our failings—not only the times when the results of our endeavours don't match our expectations, but also those occasions when we falter in our obedience to God's call. Indeed, failure is often the stepping stone we need to learn and grow—in faith as well as proficiency. Learning how to accept correction, from the Divine and the people we harm in our failings, is an important skill to develop for those who want to live vocationally.

God's grace surrounds us when we mess up. It is a safety net beneath us. It is persistent in tracking us down. But that does not mean each opportunity we receive—to do right and participate in God's healing work—is not precious and worthy of our careful discernment and timely response. God's grace, you'll remember, is not cheaply arrived at; it is the fruit of God's sacrifice and self-giving love.

www.discoverment.org

Let us therefore be good stewards of the opportunities that come our way, knowing full well that God's grace has our back, and empowers us to act boldly, risking failure for the sake of the world.

Questions for Reflection:

Share the story of a time when you experienced failure. What was it that let you down? How did you feel? Who did you tell? How has that failure helped shape your sense of who you are?

Have you ever had the results of your efforts look like failure, but still been proud of what you put into it? How do you respond to the idea that "nothing you do for the Lord is ever useless?"

Have you ever run from God's call? What did you sense God was asking of you? What about it felt like it was asking too much? How did your experience shape or effect your relationship with God?

When have you learned from a failure? What new wisdom do you carry because of it? Is it easier to learn from an experience of failing God or failing others? How do you process receiving correction?

My Daily Discoverment

MY DISCOVERMENT JOURNEY: HOW DO I MAKE DECISIONS?

Use this space to journal about any feelings, questions, or discoverments that came to you as you considered your decision-making in this section.

www.discoverment.org

My Daily Discoverment

How do I live the decisions I make?

Reflecting the character of God every day
Days 37 – 40

My Daily Discoverment

****

SET YOUR INTENTION: HOW DO I LIVE INTO THE DECISIONS I MAKE?

In this final section of reflections, I want to encourage you to consider how you inhabit the decisions you make. Making decisions is hard, but the work continues as we experience all the feelings, doubts, affirmations, and regrets that echo around us as we live into our decisions. So it's important to consider how we live a life of integrity and wholeness on the other side of our decisions.

Just as God is with us in our discerning and decision-making, so too does God walk with us in the afterglow of our decisions and in the approach to whatever new decisions will greet us. Can we recognize God in those moments? Could it be that how we live into our decisions—choosing to reflect God's character or not—is often as important as the decisions we make and the work we choose to pursue in our lives?

Consider:

- What does it mean to live a life of integrity or wholeness? Who are the people who model this for you?
- What does it look like to reflect the character of God in everyday circumstances, even circumstances that are hard?
- What aspects of God's character come natural to you? What parts of God's character are opportunities for you to grow into?

Let's Pray:

Holy One, God with us, you know what it is to live as one of us. In Jesus you inhabited moments of great consequence, and moments of mundanity. And in it all, you were without sin. Help me inhabit the moments of my life in ways that honour my belovedness and the belovedness of others. Help me reflect your character in all the decisions I make. I pray in Christ. Amen.

www.discoverment.org

****

DAY 37

Practice Good Posture

Trust in the LORD with all your heart and lean
not on your own understanding;

Proverbs 3:5 (NIV)

If you've got time to lean, you've got time to clean.

This was one of the favourite sayings of the manager at the fast food restaurant I worked at as a teenager. I admit, it's a pretty good line, and it got used quite frequently. A lot of my high school friends worked at that restaurant as well, so each after-school or weekend shift was equal parts work and socializing for us. It was a lot of fun, though I know we drove our manager to frustration with all of the leaning, and chatting, and overall slacking we did. And I imagine it didn't look very professional to the customers, seeing us lolly-gagging around so frequently.

Leaning. Slouching. Shuffling along, all hunched over. This has been my default body language, I realize, for much of my life, perhaps due to too many Gen-X slacker movies in my formative years. I'm beginning to realize how my body language reveals something about my attitude, my assumptions, and my engagement with the world that I'm not particularly proud of. I sense that my leaning and slouching communicates aloofness, disengagement, that I'm a passenger, a taker, protected by privilege, and it acts as a defense against my own failures and other's expectations of me. Now that I'm getting older, the effects of my bad posture are beginning to be felt, in the aches and pains of my aging body, and I wonder how many other areas of my life as well.

Conversely, let me tell you of a colleague of mine—a wonderful community leader—who I initially found off-putting because he walked with perfect posture wherever he went. His way of carrying himself conveyed a confidence that I thought couldn't be real and had to dismiss, much to my discredit. As I got to know him and his story, I began to realize that his way of being in the world—straight back, chin held high, a foot taller (it seemed) than anyone else in the room—was a defiant proclamation against the voices in his life that had tried to tear him down. He had come to Canada as a young adult, fleeing violence in his homeland, and had lived the immigrant experience in this land with all the micro-aggressions and open hostilities that are too frequently inflicted on new Canadians. Being around this leader challenged me to question the ways I read people, to stand up a little straighter in some areas of my own life, and to lean less on my assumptions and privilege.

How do you carry yourself as you walk through this world? What does it say about your character, your calling, and the community you feel called to serve?

It matters. Not just our body posture, but our heart posture as well. For just as our vocation is merely an idea until it finds expression in an opportunity, so too does the potential of each opportunity only get realized in our day to day, bodily and attitudinal engagement with the world around us. It does the world no good if I can articulate my vocation and walk into a meaningful opportunity, and still show up to work every day—or engage my various callings—with a crabby spirit and a miserable outlook. I'd be of more use to my community and to God's purposes, being in a less-than-ideal situation with the right attitude and an open heart. That's why, in his first letter to the Corinthians, Paul writes:

> *If I speak in the tongues of men or of angels, but do not have love, I am only a resounding gong or a clanging cymbal. If I have the gift of prophecy and can fathom all mysteries and all knowledge, and if I have a faith that can move mountains, but do not have love, I am nothing. If I give all I possess to the poor and give over my body to hardship that I may boast, but do not have love, I gain nothing. (1 Cor. 13:1-3)*

Your heart posture makes all the difference between a calling fulfilled, and an opportunity missed.

One of my wonderful colleagues at the University of Guelph teaches Vogue dance classes as part of their work supporting the LGBTQ2IA+ community on campus. Vogue dance, if you haven't seen it, features a series of stark poses and fluid movements, inspired by the posture of fashion models, that convey fierceness and carve out space for marginalized peoples. It's amazing to see really great Vogue dancers showcasing their hand work, cat walks, duck walks, and death drops—and even more impressive to think about what all these poses, postures and movements mean and proclaim to the world. I believe these dancers offer a challenge for how we carry ourselves in the world, both in our bodies and in our hearts.

What might it look like to inhabit a posture that expresses love for yourself? Strike that pose and call it Dignity.

What might it look like to inhabit a posture that expresses love for others? Strike that pose and call it Openness. Strike it again and call it Compassion.

What might it look like to inhabit a posture that expresses a love of God? Strike that pose and call it Prayer. Strike it again and call it Praise. Strike it again and call it Good Stewardship.

Whatever we are called to do, wherever we are called to serve, may we be people who project God's love into the world. May the hope that we affirm in our hearts be written on our bodies for all to see—not only in the big decisions of life, but in each day's little and ordinary moments as well.

Questions for Reflection:

Take a moment to check in with your body. Start at your toes and work your way up, flexing or stretching or moving your joints as you go. What is your body telling you as you pay attention to each part? Give thanks to God for your body. It may not be "perfect" or exactly how you'd wish it to be, but it is the gift through which God is calling you to bless the world. That's pretty awesome.

What have you been leaning on that maybe you'd like to let go of? What keeps you from letting go? Where might you draw strength and support from instead? What do the things we lean on say about our character, our faith, and our hope for the world?

What is the difference between over-confidence and dignity? How do we protect and affirm our own dignity without seeming arrogant or brash? How do we protect and affirm the dignity of the people around us, without overstepping?

How do you remember to make the most of each moment? Why is it important to stay grounded in the present moment, even as we discern and seek God for our future?

DAY 38

Get Rhythm

> "Are you tired? Worn out? Burned out on religion? Come to me. Get away with me and you'll recover your life. I'll show you how to take a real rest. Walk with me and work with me—watch how I do it. Learn the unforced rhythms of grace. I won't lay anything heavy or ill-fitting on you. Keep company with me and you'll learn to live freely and lightly."

Matthew 11:28-30 (MSG)

There are few things in life more consistent than the bass line in an old Johnny Cash song.

Boomp - Bomp. Boomp - Bomp. Boomp - Bomp. Boomp - Bomp. It pulses through the air like a heartbeat.

Boomp - Bap. Boomp - Bap. Boomp - Bomp. Boomp - Bomp. It chugs along like a train on the tracks.

If my life could be as steady as that upright bass in the Tennessee Three, I feel like nothing could ever shake me or make me come undone.

One of my favourite old Johnny Cash songs is called "Get Rhythm." Track it down on the Internet somewhere and give it a listen. In it, Cash marvels at the unflappable joy expressed by a young shoe shiner as he goes about his grimy work. The key, the young entrepreneur declares, to finding joy while serving others, is to get rhythm. Finding your rhythm is an important part of staving off the blues in those difficult moments of our vocational life.

Now I must admit, the churches I grew up in were not particularly known for having a strong sense of rhythm. There's a reason why we didn't clap very often to the music in our worship. Nevertheless, there are two elements of rhythm that I think are important for inhabiting the moments of our vocational life: patterns and practice.

Rhythms are all about patterns. Rhythms repeat. Good rhythms establish patterns of repetition and then use those patterns as a launchpad for improvisation and creativity. How well do you recognize the patterns of your vocational life—moments of searching and finding, purpose and doubt, contentment and holy unrest? How early do you begin to recognize patterns, to catch the rhythms, in the vocational seasons of your life? Can you begin to recognize them as they unfold, so you can lean into them with purpose, intentionality, and creativity?

Sometimes it takes a bunch of life experience, discernment, and reflection upon your experiences to catch hold of the vocational patterns in your life—so it's important to get lots of practice. Practice discernment. Practice your vocation. Practice your faith in ways that don't expect perfection. Be good to yourself, rely on God's grace, and you'll get better as you go. Experiment and commit yourself to a life of spiritual practices, and see if a rhythm of grace begins to emerge.

In The Message paraphrase of the Bible, Jesus invites us to "learn the unforced rhythms of grace." In more traditional translations, Jesus uses an agrarian image, inviting us to take on a yoke—a life's work—that is easy, and a burden that is light. That doesn't mean there won't be hard moments or that we should avoid life's challenges. The work we are called to, the opportunities that open up to us, may be difficult and grimy and hard. It will involve bending low in service to others. At the same time, the most important work we do, in partnership with God for the healing of the world, is not meant to feel forced or burdensome all the time. It should put a song in our hearts. Or maybe more aptly—when we choose to sing a steady song of faith with our lives, we (like the shoe shiner in Cash's song) can serve with a rhythmic and contagious joy, even in the midst of mundanity and other discouraging moments.

Are you rhythmically challenged? No worries. Jesus longs to teach us—to show us how to find the steady bass line in our lives, to reveal the song that is ours to sing.

Thanks be to God.

Questions for Reflection:

Is there a song that speaks to your experience of vocational searching these days? What is it? Why do you think it resonates for you? What does the rhythm of your chosen song stir up within you?

Why might someone working a so-called "menial" job, get the blues? What pressures face people who experience precarious employment? What gives a person dignity in their work?

www.discoverment.org

Take a few moments to do an Internet search of Ego Brown, the Washington DC shoeshine businessman who won a civil rights decision, allowing people in his trade to use public space. National newspapers ran stories on him through different parts of his career. What gives Ego Brown his dignity? How does he serve others? How do you think Ego Brown feels about his work? How does he handle discouragement?

The bass is often seen as the steady foundation that allows the rest of the band to focus on improvisation and melody. What is a steady presence in your life of faith?

My Daily Discovermen

TOTAL PRAISE
by Alydia Smith

Musicians are always aware of how music changes us physically—our hearing aids, calloused fingers, split lips, or bruised body parts often give us away. How music changes and strengthens us spiritually and emotionally may not be as obvious. The song "Total Praise" by Richard Smallwood, has transformed me by reminding me, in difficult moments, of my desire, and call, to be like Miriam.

My personal call to ministry is a conviction to do what I can to bring about God's kin-dom of justice, peace, and love on earth, like Miriam. I imagine her quietly saving her brother Moses' life, supporting, nurturing, and equipping his ministry, and then loudly praising God with a tambourine—there is no such thing as a quiet tambourine—in the wilderness when the time is right.

A couple of years ago, I was the liturgical reflector (meaning I provided worship and spiritual practices) for a delegation of the Council for World Mission in Birmingham, Alabama, which was preparing a report on the legacy of the transatlantic slave trade. The sun was disrespectfully hot and unforgiving, as we stood at countless memorials recounting how "good Christian folk" terrorized, lynched, enslaved, and murdered my ancestors. I was tired physically, emotionally, and spiritually. I could not imagine how any prayer, ritual, or liturgical action could do anything at all to combat the monstrous evil of racism. I felt trapped in a scorching wilderness experience unsure if I was capable to do what was being asked of me.

I sat in my hotel room, overwhelmed to the point where all I could do was look up. It was then that the words of the psalmist, "I lift mine eyes unto the hills," came to me, accompanied by the song "Total Praise." It reminded me of Miriam pulling out her tambourine in the wilderness, and it became my struggle (or fight) song. It is the song I turn to when times are rough, I doubt my ability to live out my calling, and I need some spiritual courage to stay and fight for God's kin-dom instead of run away. It draws on my spiritual tradition in its unapologetically gospel sound, and the music beautifully holds the tension that I feel as I work out how I am going to fight through whatever adversity is in my way, while also staying true to my highest calling: to give all glory and praise to God through the bringing-about of God's kin-dom.

Throughout my spiritual journey I have had many fight songs, from "How Great Thou Art" to "Sleepers Awake". I always make sure that I have a spiritual song on-the-ready to help nurture and strengthen my soul until I am ready to pick up my tambourine, like Miriam, and praise God loudly.

DAY 39

God's Providence

> Therefore I tell you, do not worry about your life, what you
> will eat or drink; or about your body, what you will wear.
> Is not life more than food, and the body more than clothes?
> Look at the birds of the air; they do not sow or reap or store
> away in barns, and yet your heavenly Father feeds them.
>
> Matthew 6:25-26a (NIV)

Adulting is hard.

When I was a teenager, with a paper route and annoying teachers and family rules to follow, I thought 22 would be the perfect age. You'd be able to go out whenever you wanted, stay up really late with friends and eat whatever you wanted from your own refrigerator.

When I was 22, with vocational uncertainty and tuition to pay and no significant other, I thought my 30s would be the perfect decade for me. I'd be established in a career, laying down roots, and maybe even with a family of my own.

Now that I'm past both of those markers, I'm realizing that every stage of life has its own challenges, struggles, and joys. The needs of a child or a teenager are just as serious and important as the needs of an adult or a senior. And while yes, the needs that an adult may need to juggle—bills, children, career, parents, partners, etc.—are significant, there is also the added benefit of being able to look back and see God's faithfulness over past experiences.

When my wife and I get stewing about precarious employment, or what's best for our children, or other big life decisions, we usually fall back on a simple saying: God's been good to us this far. It might sound simplistic, but I'm glad we can look back and see God's faithfulness to us in times both joyous and challenging.

The word providence is what we typically use in the church to describe God's sustaining care of us. It comes from the verb "to provide", which itself comes from two Latin words: "pro" which means forward or on behalf of, and "vide" which means to see. It affirms that God will see to our various needs as they come up. Furthermore, God sees us in our different places of need, and responds.

The challenge is sometimes whether we will see God at work in our lives or not. Having trust in God's providence is a whole lot easier when we can be open to seeing the ways God provides for us physically, emotionally, spiritually, and more.

Anyone who's taken a first-year psychology course will likely be familiar with Maslow's hierarchy of needs. It's the idea that we all carry and tend to different levels of needs in our lives. First there are physical needs (food, shelter, sleep, etc.) and safety needs (security, health, employment, etc.), then belonging needs (friendship, intimacy, connection), esteem needs (respect, recognition, etc.), and self-actualization. According to this hierarchy, a person must satisfy their base needs before they move on to the higher or more conceptual needs.

The problem is that we sometimes get stuck building storehouses for our base needs, and never move up the pyramid to consider or tend to our more conceptual needs. Yes, we need paycheques and a roof over our heads, but we also need to find meaning in our work and to feel like we are part of something bigger than ourselves.

I pray that God will see to your material needs, providing things like a paycheque and work and a roof over your head. It may not be glamorous, but hopefully it is sufficient, like the manna that fell from the sky and sustained the Israelites in the wilderness. Beyond that, I pray God will also provide you with a sense of vocational calling.

I pray that God will see to your spiritual needs, providing you with answers to some of your deep longings. Additionally, I pray God will also provide you with deeper questions, drawing you into a more robust, dynamic and truthful relationship with yourself and God and the world.

Adulting is hard. Our needs are real. But we belong to a God who engages with hard things and sees us in our need. Thanks be to our God, who provides.

Questions for Reflection:

How do you respond to the idea that "adulting" is hard? What has proven harder than you thought? What hardship can you see on the horizon? What barriers and imbalanced systems make "adulting" even harder on some than it is on others?

When have you felt "seen" by someone, in a moment of need? What did that make possible in your interactions with them? When have you felt unseen by someone you really needed that from? What resulted from that missed opportunity?

How do you respond to Maslow's hierarchy of needs? Is it a helpful way to conceptualize and prioritize our needs? How might you reimagine it better?

Jesus tells us not to worry about the things of our life—what we will eat, drink, wear, etc. Do you worry about those things? What do you worry about? What does worrying do for you and within you? How might you transform your worry into something a little more helpful? If you could be freed from worry, what might you be released to pursue?

DAY 40

Producing Good Fruit

> The acts of the flesh are obvious… But the fruit of the Spirit is love, joy, peace, forbearance, kindness, goodness, faithfulness, gentleness and self-control. Against such things there is no law.
>
> Galatians 5:19a, 22-23 (NIV)

One of the common refrains I hear as a campus minister is the regret, shame, and defeat that students express regarding their lack of productivity. There is just so much to do! So much that I have to produce before the next due date. I have to read so many pages. I have to write so many papers. I have to pull up my grade or I can't possibly come to worship with you, or join others for coffee, or go out for a walk or tend to my mental health… it's just not productive.

I will admit, the demands of the academic system are ridiculous. Universities and colleges expect things that are beyond what normal people should be able to produce. And the costs involved—in tuition and otherwise—make academic study a high stakes game that seems to leave little wiggle room for failure or well-being.

But the reality is, the world outside of academia isn't much different. We are all measured by how much we produce—whether it's the number of widgets coming off the assembly line, the amount of content being pumped into a social media feed, the bums in the pews in a ministry context, or the value we generate for our shareholders and investors. Even parents, doing the work of raising children and nurturing a home, can get caught up in the desire to produce highly accomplished children and promote the image of perfect parenthood. Whatever field of work we are in, if we're not producing enough, we begin to question (or others question for us) the value of our work, if not the value of our personhood.

And the worst part is, in our consumer society, the messaging we receive is that there is never "enough." The answer to how much we should produce is always "more." Technologies that were supposed to make work life easier and free up more time have simply led to higher demands and to the expectation that workers can be productive even from home or while they're on holidays. If we play the productivity game, we always lose. We can never produce enough to satisfy the world.

But scripture gives us a different vision of productivity.

When we are living into our vocational calling, when we are participating in God's redemptive work of healing and bringing wholeness to the world, our productivity isn't measured in things you can count—not even in souls saved or oppressions vanquished, though there are many Christians who like to tally such things. When John was preaching in Galilee, preparing the people for the ministry of Jesus, he told the powerful of his day, "Produce fruit in keeping with repentance. And do not think you can say to yourselves, 'We have Abraham as our father. I tell you that out of these stones God can raise up children for Abraham" (Matthew 3:8-9 NIV). God doesn't need us to produce in the way that employers or professors or consumer society demands of us.

Instead, the good fruit we produce in a life of vocational living are things like love, joy, peace, forbearance, kindness, goodness, faithfulness, gentleness, and self-control. You might know them as the Fruit of the Spirit. Qualities. Qualities growing within us. Qualities that reflect the character of God. Qualities, not born from our effort or abilities, but from our openness to the Spirit's work within us. We know we are producing what we should, when we see God's character growing in our lives and spilling over into the world around us.

As we inhabit the moments of our days and live into the decisions we make about work, family, school, etc. may we see the Fruit of the Spirit growing up from our lives. May we be rooted in God's vision of justice, attune to the presence of God around and within us, and may we pour ourselves out as Jesus did, so the Spirit of the Living God may pour in and through us into the world.

My Daily Discoverment

Questions for Reflection:

Where do you feel the demands towards productivity in your life? Where does that pressure come from? What is behind it? How do you respond to it? Where do you see the demands of productivity creeping into the Church or your own personal faith life?

What does it mean to produce fruit in keeping with repentance? What does repentance have to do with what we produce in the world?

The Fruit of the Spirit are: love, joy, peace, forbearance, kindness, goodness, faithfulness, gentleness, and self-control. Which of these do you see evidence of in your life? Which of these are you hoping to cultivate more of? What does it mean that these are fruit born of the Spirit, not fruit of our efforts or productivity?

How open are you to the Holy Spirit at work within you? What is comforting about that idea? What is uncomfortable about it? What might allowing the Spirit more leeway to shape you look like in your life? If it feels right, consider inviting the Holy Spirit to work in you and through you right now.

MY DISCOVERMENT JOURNEY: HOW DO I LIVE INTO THE DECISIONS I MAKE?

Use this space to journal about any feelings, questions, or discoverments that came to you as you considered your living in this section.

www.discoverment.org

A Final Blessing and Commission

Get on with it!

A FINAL BLESSING AND COMMISSION—GET ON WITH IT!

> Peace be with you! As the Father has sent me, I am sending you. John 20:21 (NIV)

Doubt is a steady companion of faith, discernment, and loving action. Perhaps it has been following you as you've engaged in this process. Perhaps it still lingers, even now, in ways that challenge or confound or disappoint you. Expect doubt to be a steady companion throughout your vocational life.

One of the voices that I turn to frequently in my own moments of doubt and discernment is that of Canadian theologian Douglas John Hall. His book, *Why Christian?* is an imagined discourse between himself and a young adult, someone on the edge of faith. In it, he describes his response to the doubt that mocks and belittles him—asking "What makes you think you can do justice to this?"—whenever he engages a piece of work he feels called to. Hall writes:

> *And then I have to say to myself: "But my work, unimpressive as it may be, is only a small part of the visible tip of a labour—God's labour—that is infinitely greater. Moreover,"* I add, *"this is the work to which I have been beckoned. God permits it, and God will do with it what God wills. So please, my dear sir: Get on with it!"* (Hall, p. 107)

God is sending us into the world, to participate in the healing of Creation, to take up a piece of God's redemptive labour, to discover our true selves and to offer our lives in the service of others. Make no mistake. God is sending you—the real you—with all your limitations, failures, misgivings, and doubts.

Furthermore, there is a whole community of people—past and present—standing with you, who express the same confidence as the apostle Paul, "that the one who began a good work among you will bring it to completion" (Philippians 1:6).

So get on with it. Be guided by the Spirit. Be confident in who you are becoming. Seek forgiveness and grace when you need it—both are in abundant supply. Find partners and community and wise counsel—you do not have to go it alone. Be open to God's call and the discoverments God reveals to you on the way. And be at peace—with yourself and with God and the world.

But do get on with it.

Life awaits—the real life you were made for. Can you hear it calling?

WORKS CITED

Benner, David. *The Gift of Being Yourself.* InterVarsity Press, 2004.

Bojaxhiu, Teresa. "Mother Teresa Reflects on Working Toward Peace." Santa Clara University, https://www.scu.edu/mcae/architects-of-peace/Teresa/essay.html. Accessed 23 March 2021.

Bonhoeffer, Dietrich. *The Cost of Discipleship.* Simon and Schuster, 1995.

Buechner, Frederick. *Wishful Thinking: A Seeker's ABC.* HarperOne, 1993.

Cash, Johnny. "Get Rhythm." *The Essential Johnny Cash*, Legacy/Columbia, 2002.

Daniel, Lillian, and Martin B. Copenhaver. *This Odd and Wondrous Calling.* Wm. B. Eerdman's Publishing Company, 2009.

Dean, Kenda Creasy. *Practicing Passion—Youth and the Quest for a Passionate Church.* Wm. B. Eerdman's Publishing Company, 2004.

Dylan, Bob. "Everything is Broken." *Oh Mercy*, Columbia, 1989.

Epstein, David. *Range: Why Generalists Triumph in a Specialized World.* Riverhead Books, 2019.

Faber, Frederick W. "There's a Wideness in God's Mercy." http://www.hymntime.com/tch/htm/t/h/e/r/w/therwide.htm. Accessed 23 March 2021.

Foster, Richard. *Celebration of Discipline.* Harper & Row, 1988.

Gorman, Michael. *Abide and Go: Missional Theosis in the Gospel of John.* Cascade Books, 2018.

Guder, Darrell. *Missional Church.* Wm. B. Eerdman's Publishing Company, 1998.

Hall, Douglas John. *Why Christian?* Fortress Press, 1998.

King Jr., Martin Luther. "The Other America." http://www.gphistorical.org/mlk/mlkspeech/mlk-gp-speech.pdf. Accessed 23 March 2021.

Lewis, C.S. *The Lion, The Witch and The Wardrobe*. Lions, 1988.

Liebert, Elizabeth. *The Way of Discernment—Spiritual Practices for Decision Making*. Westminster John Knox Press, 2008.

Merton, Thomas. *Thoughts in Solitude*. Farrar, Straus and Giroux, 1999.

Neafsey, John. *A Sacred Voice is Calling*. Orbis Books, 2006.

Nouwen, Henri. *Discernment*. HarperOne, 2013.

Nouwen, Henri. *Life of the Beloved*. The Crossroad Publishing Company, 2002.

Ortberg, John. *All the Places to Go*. Tyndale House Publishers Inc., 2015.

Placher, William C., editor. *Callings—Twenty Centuries of Christian Wisdom on Vocation*. Wm. B. Eerdman's Publishing Company, 2005.

"Pajama Party." *Pee-wee's Playhouse*, created by Paul Reubens, season 2, episode 10, CBS, 1987.

Rowling, J.K. *Harry Potter and the Chamber of Secrets*. Bloomsbury, 2014.

Singer, Peter. *The Most Good You Can Do—How Effective Altruism is Changing Ideas About Living Ethically*. Yale University Press, 2015.

"Song of Faith." *The United Church of Canada*, 2006, https://united-church.ca/community-faith/welcome-united-church-canada/faith-statements. Accessed 23 March 2021.

Taylor, Barbara Brown. *An Altar in the World*. Harper One, 2009.

Thurman, Howard. *The Living Wisdom of Howard Thurman*. Sounds True, 2010. Audiobook.

Watson, Lilla. "Lilla Watson > Quotes." https://www.goodreads.com/quotes/844825. Accessed 23 March 2021.

Watts, Isaac. "When I Survey the Wondrous Cross." https://hymnary.org/text/when_i_survey_the_wondrous_cross_watts. Accessed 23 March 2021.

Willard, Dallas. *Hearing God*. InterVarsity Press Books, 2012.

www.discoverment.org

GRATITUDE AND THANKS

I want to extend my thanks to all the mentors, ministers, parents, and elders who helped place this workbook in your hands. Without the encouragement of our communities, the task of vocational discernment would be a difficult and lonely endeavour.

Thanks to you, for taking the time to engage this resource, for your patience in the pages that might've fallen flat, and for the investment you're making in your careful discernment. I can't wait to see the fruit of your callings.

Thanks to the Vision Fund of the United Church of Canada for making the development of this resource possible, and to all those who support United Church Mission and Service. Also to the Forum for Theological Exploration for helping launch the initial phase of this project, some years ago.

Much gratitude for the contributors to this workbook and all those with whom I've been fortunate enough to discuss, explore, and bounce around ideas of vocational discernment with over the years. Big thanks especially to Karen Orr, Bronwyn Corlett, and Robin McGauley for their passion, creativity and commitment to this work. Gratitude to Thomas Littlewood for his editing, and Jordana Wright for her coaching and encouragement.

I am indebted to the students, board members, and ministry partners of the Ecumenical Campus Ministry at the University of Guelph. I feel blessed to be called to serve alongside you. Can't wait to see how the Spirit might continue to move among us.

Thanks indeed, to the centuries upon centuries of Indigenous stewards of the land upon which we live and work and discern our futures.

And of course, thanks and praise to the God of all. It is all grace. What a joy it is to serve our God!